LA
RE:

Contents

Prologue
An LA story: how it all began

Chapter 1 - Introduction
What makes LA special?

Chapter 2 - Media, Entertainment & Music
Viva Hollywood – beating heart of media, music and entertainment

Chapter 3 - Gaming
LA's got game

Chapter 4 - Retail
The changing shape of retail

Chapter 5 - Health & Wellness
Looking good, feeling great

Chapter 6 - Food
The future of food, now

Chapter 7 - Transport
Navigating Los Angeles and beyond

Conclusion
So where next?

Prologue

An LA story: how it all began

It was on a cold winter's evening in our London apartment in March 2015 that my partner and I decided on a new adventure. We were going to head 5,500 miles west to California and the City of Angels, joining ten million other people in that vast metropolis of possibility.

Back then, I have to admit, Los Angeles wasn't high on my list of cities I wanted to spend time in. However, after speaking to people who knew it well and having done some research into the city, I became more and more intrigued by it.

I've always considered myself a citizen of the world, and my career in the news media has enabled me to be so. A native Londoner, my career started with Trinity Mirror, managing Interactive for the group's national newspapers - think of it as mobile before smart phones came out (we were ahead of the game!). I moved to Paris in 2006 to satisfy my curiosity about living in another country and to learn another language, and ended up staying for almost six years.

After joining a media non-profit where I wrote about innovation in the news industry and helped grow the profitability of their annual summit of 1500+ news executives, I was approached by the New York Times to work on the European syndication and licensing business. I found myself travelling across Europe meeting editors and publishers to launch partnerships with the New York Times, all possible thanks to the best team I have ever built.

Five years later, leaving the New York Times was a tough decision but I was ready for a change.

It was 2013 and social media was booming. Technology and 'the cloud' were becoming increasingly more important in business strategies. With my expertise in media, both business and editorial, I wanted to work with technology-focused businesses. I spent the next four years as a strategist for multiple media and early-stage technology organisations.

When the idea of Los Angeles came up in 2015, I was keen to know all about a new technology being developed there: Virtual Reality (VR). The 'godmother of VR', LA-based Nonny de la Peña, took me under her wing and showed me her early work. It was a profound experience, being strapped into a headset, feeling long wires dragging behind me which linked me to a high-end computer.

All of a sudden I found myself in a rudimentary version of a Syrian street with real audio, witnessing a street bomb explosion and the ensuing chaos.

Immediately I recognised the long-term potential for news and storytelling to be able to take people to new worlds from the comfort of their living rooms.

By 2017 I was witnessing other innovative technologies in Los Angeles with huge potential for media businesses: live streaming, social video, storytelling across platforms, on-demand TV, interactivity and in-app commerce. I wanted to share all this with my European network.

With my dual networks of US innovators and thought leaders and international media executives, I set up FORE:media, connecting them all so they could improve and future-proof their businesses.

One thing puzzled me: almost every executive I spoke to wanted to visit Silicon Valley. It was a badge of honour to visit what has been seen as the home of technology and innovation; it demonstrated to peers back home in the UK or Europe that you were looking ahead and must therefore have an understanding of future technology.

However, knowing the specifics of what these executives were looking for, most of the innovative businesses were actually in Los Angeles. Yet LA couldn't boast that same badge of honour - when it came to business and innovation, it simply wasn't on people's radars.

The city can be inscrutable to those who don't know it - there is no city centre but instead a vast network of towns and smaller cities. Los Angeles does not spend a lot of time on its own public relations, so many people in Europe and outside the States don't realise that it's the second biggest city in the US, with a GDP of more than $1 trillion which is up 40% since 2001 (by comparison, San Francisco is half that at $500 billion), that more than $6.4 billion was raised in the city in venture funding in 2018, or that Los Angeles is the most productive of the five largest cities in the US.

Perhaps it's not that people misunderstand Los Angeles, but that they don't know what LA has become.

And so I wrote this book to take you on a journey to the heart of this invigorating city, introducing you to the executives who have made it their home and the base for their work. You'll get to know their diverse industries and, in so doing, you will join me in understanding why LA rocks when it comes to innovation.

Book-ended by some of the incredible innovations in LA's two oldest industries - Hollywood and aerospace - you'll also find out how a 15 year-old boy took a simple family recipe and turned it into a $600 million industry; how a follicly-challenged CEO built a personalised hair dye company that has taken the world by storm; which company really invented the drive-thru (clue: it wasn't McDonalds) and why the number 405 can be used as a swear word.

And, because we're all short of time, I've given you the TL;DR version at the end of each chapter so you can sound smart after a quick read. You're welcome!

A side note on innovation

So what exactly is innovation? The definition according to the Oxford English Dictionary is: the introduction of new things, ideas or ways of doing something.

Innovation culture doesn't belong to one city alone. Silicon Valley is renowned as the origin of big tech which has radically changed our lives, and Israel can boast more startups and venture capitalists per capita than any other country. London's cultural diversity and proximity to mainland Europe have led to a startup ecosystem colloquially known as 'Silicon Roundabout', and there are innovation hubs in Austin, Detroit, Seattle and many other cities around the world.

My view is that the term 'innovation' is so overused that it has become a misnomer. Here are some things that innovation is NOT:

- Innovation is nuanced. There is not one single definition of it. Removing office walls and adding a ping-pong table might improve inter-company communications but it won't suddenly make that company more innovative.

- Innovation means different things to different people. It can happen through incremental change, as well as being something that will have a major impact on the future of homo sapiens.

- Innovation isn't always about technology. A burger was the most unexpected innovation at the giant CES (Consumer Electronics Show) in January 2019. The Impossible Burger is vegan, grown entirely in a lab - mostly from soy - yet indistinguishable from a conventional burger [1].

- Successful innovation means failing, usually more than once. For evidence, try Googling 'Einstein's Mistakes' or go to the Museum of Failure to see some spectacular flops from the world's greatest brands.

[1] Engadget Best of CES Awards 2019

Introduction to Los Angeles

What makes LA special?

Los Angeles has become a major force in innovation. In fact it's the creative innovation capital of the world. A bold statement, I know.

How did this happen? In part because Hollywood's legendary storytelling roots have intertwined with technology to make the city the world's biggest creative innovation hub.

In turn new social media influencers - who often have a much larger following than traditional celebrities – have become 21st century 'publishers', attracting bigger and bigger advertising budgets. An influencer with a million followers can earn $100,000 for a single post on Instagram.

Media giants are innovating with exciting new business models by going straight to digital. The lines are blurring between traditional studios such as Disney and DreamWorks, and new well-funded entrants. After all, media companies are all competing for the same thing: your time and attention.

Los Angeles is more ethnically diverse than many other cities, and in that sense it outstrips Silicon Valley. There is even a joke that no one actually comes from Los Angeles. More than 200 languages are spoken by the 10 million+ inhabitants of the city and because there is no dominating demographic, this rich cultural diversity is embodied in the creativity of the products and services being forged there.

In fact, Los Angeles is now the fastest-growing startup ecosystem in the entire US, with the highest number of people starting a new business every month.[2]

For years, business executives from all over the world have been making pilgrimages to Silicon Valley to try to understand the basis for the innovation that has taken place there. But if you look closely, it was technology that was developed there. To some degree it still is, especially B2B services and hardware.

[2] LAEDC

Photo credit: Philip Pilosian / Shutterstock.com

Introduction to Los Angeles

Mayor Eric Garcetti
@MayorOfLA

It's a #SpaceX Falcon 9 launch from Vandenberg Air Force Base.

But technology is being developed everywhere now and affects every single business, meaning that new innovation comes from technology at the intersection of other businesses and industries. This takes a creative, open mind-set – something at which LA happens to excel. It's a city of collaboration, of diversity that doesn't concern itself with what the neighbours think; it just wants to create awesome things, and to enjoy doing it.

Just as Silicon Valley is now the 'tech' town, Hollywood has long been Los Angeles' most famous and enduring industry – one which brings a staggering $161 billion each year to the economy.

But the city isn't a one-trick pony: it has a rich history of innovation in other diverse areas of enterprise. Take space exploration. LA is home to NASA's Research and Development Centre and the Jet Propulsion Laboratory which developed America's first earth-orbiting science satellite and created the first successful interplanetary spacecraft. Northrup Grumman's 110-acre campus, just south of the airport, houses their most innovative and influential aerospace designs. And SpaceX, probably the most prominent private space company - owned and run by Elon Musk – sometimes surprises the city's residents with unannounced spaceship launches, fuelling excited speculation about UFOs and panicked posts on social media about nuclear attack.

Los Angeles' credentials as an innovative powerhouse don't stop there. It is also the Number One manufacturing centre in the US, producing more in LA County than in the majority of most other entire states (42 to be precise).

LA also has a vast leisure and tourism industry (with 29.4 million hotel nights sold per annum), while successful companies originating in the city in recent years include Ring (the home video doorbell sold to Amazon and now grown into a home security company), Bird (a dockless electric scooter-sharing company and the fastest company to reach a $1 billion valuation), Snapchat (the social media phenomenon for millennials), Riot Games (the video game developer and esports company) and Dollar Shave Club (a subscription shaving club sold to Unilever for $1 billion in 2016).

Historically much of the venture capital money has been in Silicon Valley, but this is shifting too. At the beginning of 2019, the number of VC firms in Los Angeles had grown to 104. There were also 33 accelerators, 43 incubators and 73 co-working spaces supporting the more than 1,145+ active startups that call Los Angeles their home. In 2017 alone, 300 of these companies received external funding, and 80 more sold majority stakes - or sold up entirely - to larger companies.

So as the world starts to question its love affair with Silicon Valley, asking whether the technology startups we once worshipped are benefiting us or harming us as they have grown into giants, the city to the south, the one with the sunshine, the laid-back attitude and the booming economy, is taking its place.

In 2017, the creative industries employed more than 500,000 workers in Los Angeles County, making it the largest centre for the creative industries in the US.

A creative industries worker in Los Angeles County was paid almost double the countywide average wage in 2017, at $109,000 per year compared with $61,800.

- 2019 Otis Report on the Creative Economy

Talent magnet

There is an exceptional amount of talent already in Los Angeles thanks to outstanding universities including University of Southern California (USC), University of California Los Angeles (UCLA) and CalTech. As well as boasting the greatest number of engineering graduates in the US, there are also excellent design programmes. In fact by most metrics, LA County is home to four of the top ten design programmes in the country.

It's also easy to attract talent to Los Angeles for the exceptional lifestyle it affords.

According to the Best Places living cost comparison website, San Francisco is 56.2% more expensive than Los Angeles, with housing almost double the cost. In LA you get a lot more bang for your buck, enabling people to live in bigger homes with more outdoor space.

Having outdoor space enables Angelenos to enjoy their 292 days of sunshine every year with average temperatures of 72 degrees (that's 22 degrees to Europeans and Canadians). This year-round weather means it's possible to enjoy the 75 miles of vast local sandy beaches, as well as hiking miles of trails in the Santa Monica Mountains and Hollywood Hills.

And that's just nature in the immediate vicinity of the city. Hop in the car for a weekend escape to the wine regions around Santa Barbara; the micro-breweries of San Diego; the Mojave Desert or Joshua Tree National Park; the giant tree forests of Sequoia National Park or Mexico not far to the south. It's possible to surf and ski in the same day if you're so inclined.

Many people in LA make the most of the weather and surroundings. On the west side of the city it's not uncommon for people to go surfing before work - in fact Google provides surfboards at its Venice office. You'll often see people carrying yoga mats from their daily practice as they head to the office.

I've heard people say that LA lacks culture but this isn't true. LA has more museums and galleries per inhabitant than anywhere else in the US. Los Angeles County Museum of Art (LACMA) is the largest art museum in the western US and the Getty Museum is worth a visit for the architecture and stunning city views alone. The infamous Frieze Art Fair recently chose Los Angeles as its inaugural west coast destination.

So how does LA's social scene compare with Silicon Valley's? Many neighbourhoods in Los Angeles have excellent restaurants and bars that are buzzing at evenings and weekends, no matter whether it's Santa Monica and Venice on the Westside, West Hollywood or Downtown LA. Compare that to downtown Curpotino, Palo Alto or Sunnyvale in Silicon Valley, which are all very quiet. Los Angeles offers so much more.

With all this on the doorstep, why wouldn't you want to take advantage of this lifestyle and live in Los Angeles? It's no wonder so many people move from all over the world to this melting pot - exactly as I did.

Driving diversity, celebrating difference

To do business in Los Angeles, we need to also understand how the city is changing. One of the things I love about LA is its diversity. It's one of the most diverse cities in the US and it's also in the top ten globally, falling only slightly behind New York and London.

This diversity is accentuated by LA's sheer size: it's the second largest city in the US by both population and GDP. According to the World Population Review, LA is home to people from more than 140 countries speaking 224 languages (I didn't realise there were that many either). And only 65% of Angelenos were born in the US. It's a true melting pot.

By contrast, under-representation in Silicon Valley is one of the reasons the area has lost its shine. For the tech industry in particular, inequality is not only an ethical issue where people of colour are not represented, it's also a structural problem: how can we build products for society when the businesses producing them don't accurately reflect and understand their audience? We're now starting to feel the effects of white guys making all the product decisions in years gone by. Keyvan Peymani, someone that has branched technology, investment and entertainment companies large and small suggests that 'Facebook may not be facing the issues it is now had it been based in LA as it would have had to address the issues much earlier'.

California is an affluent state, and Los Angeles is a wealthy county with relatively high median personal earnings, particularly when compared with the rest of the United States. The white population in Los Angeles earns significantly more than the US median income.

In contrast, Latinos are the only ethnic group who earn less.[3] Yet 9% of all Hispanics in the US live in Los Angeles County, and it's here that the population has grown the most since 1980.

Population of LA County's Major Racial & Ethnic Groups

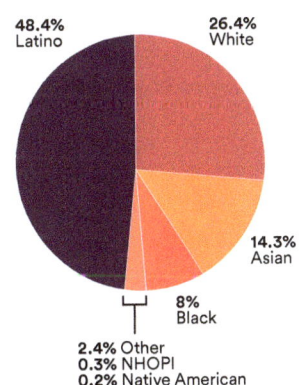

48.4% Latino
26.4% White
14.3% Asian
8% Black
2.4% Other
0.3% NHOPI
0.2% Native American

[3] US Census Bureau ACS 2015. Chart source: US Census Bureau ACS, 2015

Beatriz Acevedo, founder of video network Mitu and a celebrated Latina businesswoman with the energy of a stick of dynamite in human form (in a good way), spends a lot of her time talking about this issue and helping to educate people on the vast opportunity it brings. When we met, she explained: "Despite being the majority population in Los Angeles, Latinos are still a massive blind spot for most when it comes to the perception of them being a key demographic and proven driver of business growth."

Annual Latino population growth in Los Angeles is forecast by 2023 to be at +3.8%, while non-Latino whites will be at a decline of -1.2%.

Beatriz says: "As a CEO or businessman/woman, which one would you choose? It's baffling to see that most choose to invest the majority of their marketing dollars, funding efforts, workforce development etc. in the latter, when this clearly makes no business sense. Latinos in this town and in this country are the best investment anyone can make to 'future-proof' their business and every metric proves this. Yet deep unconscious biases prevent many top decision-makers from choosing to invest in what can be a transformational business opportunity that Latinos offer like no other cohort."

Beatriz is right - there is a huge business opportunity that isn't being addressed. Total Hispanics and all Latina age groups over-index on the purchases of health and beauty products [4], for example, while US Latinos drive approximately 70-100% of sales growth for car makers including Honda, Ford, Chevy, Hyundai and Kia [5].

Understanding changing markets is doubly important because the growth in LA is representative of the US as a whole: Latinos will account for 75% of US growth in the workforce from 2020-2034, and their median income has doubled in the last few years.

[4] The Nielsen Company 2017. [5] LAT L'Attitude.

Money, money, money

It's hard not to compare Los Angeles, to Silicon Valley when it comes to Venture Capital (VC). Silicon Valley is credited as the place where the VC industry began. It's certainly the oldest-established VC market and is still by far the largest - successful VC-backed exits of $500+ million in the last decade total a whopping $1 trillion[6].

However it's a different market to Los Angeles. Geographically speaking, Silicon Valley is a small area and, given its single industry focus around pure technology, professional and social circles are often the same - which means information flows quickly. Many companies that get funding are started by people who have some affiliation or experience with Stanford and/or top tech companies such as Google or Facebook. It's a recipe that has worked over and over again, particularly for tech companies and those focused on the B2B space.

Since 2010, the Los Angeles venture capital scene has been growing. It's a different market to Silicon Valley. The industries funded are more consumer-focused, serving media, gaming, retail, health and wellness. All of which makes sense, given the creative roots and enormous, diverse consumer market there.

Historically, because there hasn't been as much funding in LA and because entrepreneurs come from such diverse backgrounds, it's a city of underdogs who need to work harder to get where they want to be. It's a far cry from the wealthy elite in Silicon Valley who can afford to go to expensive business schools. The lack of VC funding in LA also means that startups have had to prove product that's market-fit and get to monetisation earlier than companies with VC money. These are useful skills and have stood these companies in good stead.

Talking about LA success stories, Mark Suster, Partner at Upfront Ventures which is one of LA's most established VC firms, points to a number of cases where LA startups have excelled in monetisation. Most of the companies have been snapped up by Silicon Valley giants. One example of this is Bill Gross's idea of pay-per-click advertising, also known as sponsored search, which most people didn't like when he launched it at his LA-based company GoTo.com. He sold it (then as Overture) to Yahoo for $1.6 billion in 2003, and this is now the internet's largest revenue model.

In the same year another company, Applied Semantics, which you may now know as Adsense, was bought by Google for $102 million.

[6] Founder Collective.

This Santa Monica-based company used semantics to measure and predict intent, another huge business model for the internet (and the one responsible for ads following you around your online browsing). The original price comparison websites such as PriceGrabber and Shopzilla also started in Los Angeles.

These companies all started with relatively low funding and proved their revenue models before being acquired. Silicon Valley tends to be different. William Hsu, Co-Founder of Mucker Capital, an LA-based VC who was raised in the Bay area, went to Stanford and knows Silicon Valley inside-out. He offers a car-based analogy to explain the difference:

In LA cars conserve petrol, travelling slowly until they reach the next petrol station. In Silicon Valley they go out fully loaded and at full speed. He explains that they're just different models flexing different muscles. The growth muscle - speeding in this case - can be learnt as the money comes in once the business is ready. It doesn't have to be immediate to succeed. I've heard the same thing from other local VCs such as M13, who respect the fact that companies stay under the radar for longer, making their capital go further.

There are a few VC firms betting on companies that are able to do this - from one of the earliest vocal advocates of the LA startup scene, Upfront Ventures, to newer local funds including Mucker, M13 and Amplify. In fact Mucker goes one step further. Visit their website and the first thing you will see is: *Not in Silicon Valley? Not a problem*. Based in Los Angeles, Mucker provides capital and support for startups outside Silicon Valley. These VCs all see the value in companies that don't have the elite advantage of Silicon Valley.

Now operating their fourth fund, Mucker is starting to see the rewards, as are other VCs who have taken this stance on Los Angeles. In the last decade, 14 LA companies have exited with valuations over $500 million, totalling just under $60 billion. This is significantly more than the other main startup hub outside Silicon Valley: New York.

These exits are excellent early signs for LA according to Eric Pakravan at VC firm Amplify LA. He explains that Silicon Valley has had much longer to get to where it is. It takes years to build an ecosystem, and most companies take 10+ years before they exit. Early LA companies are only starting to reach that point in the last couple of years. Eric is the man behind an annual report on the 'LA Tech and Venture Scene', and explains that it's really in the last five years that the VC market has been established with both home-grown and national VC firms having a presence in LA, which combined, service multiple startup stages. In 2009, a little over $2 billion was raised by companies in LA. In 2018 that tripled to $6.4 billion[7].

Because it is young, Los Angeles still doesn't have many of the 'tentpole' companies we know from Silicon Valley - Google, Facebook and Apple.

[7] Founder Collective.

Venture Capital in Los Angeles

Chart source: Amplify LA

It has had a lot of medium-size companies that have done well but are not instantly recognised as household names. Slowly but surely, LA companies such as Snap, Tesla, SpaceX and gaming company Riot are coming to prominence, while large tech companies like Amazon and Google are opening big offices and hiring in LA. This will, of course, have an impact on the overall ecosystem.

This more rounded VC funding landscape, combined with a maturing startup ecosystem, means LA-based companies are no longer as reliant on Silicon Valley VCs as they once were. Courtney Reum, co-founder of M13, explains that a decade ago there was a debate for founders in LA as to whether they should start their business in LA or Silicon Valley. Either way, an LA-based company would have had to travel to Silicon Valley to secure all or part of their funding.

All that has changed. With more funds, talent and executives on their second or third business with established local networks, all the resources an LA founder needs can be found locally. Travis Kalanick, the founder of Uber, is from LA but started his business in Silicon Valley because that's where the money was. However he is building his next business, Cloud Kitchens, in LA.

It's been encouraging to see more funds come to Los Angeles, fuelling business and a creative startup environment. Now the umbers are backing up the theory - Los Angeles has a booming startup ecosystem in which venture capitalists want to take part.

It's not (all) about the money

Most founders and executives I speak to in Los Angeles have a different perspective from others in the US. In Silicon Valley, startup talk is of funds raised and valuations, both of which are often used as a benchmark for whether a meeting should be taken or not. In Los Angeles it's different, perhaps because there hasn't been as much funding available and they have had to be more scrappy and reach profitability more quickly. Perhaps it's because the business world is changing. Either way, we hear founders in LA talk more about their purpose, which often encapsulates some form of social responsibility.

Take the brands on trendy Abbot Kinney Boulevard in Venice. Restaurants such as the Tasting Kitchen, Butchers Daughter, Felix and Gjelina all promote ethically-sourced food, while TOMS' entire mission centres on giving away a pair of shoes to someone in need for every pair bought.

It's difficult to quantify this 'good will' since, by standard data metrics, Los Angeles isn't top of the list for philanthropic giving or time volunteered. As Cinny Kennard, Executive Director of the Annenberg Foundation, an LA-based philanthropic foundation set up in 1989 told me: "[As Angelenos] we want to do it differently than other cities, we want to tell a different story".

After leaving LA on a project in Washington DC for two and a half years, the city she came back to in 2015 was very different. It was beginning to boom. Speaking with Wallis Annenberg, the President and Chairwoman of the Annenberg Foundation, upon her return, they agreed that they wanted to continue to help the city become the best it could be in this new chapter so that as it evolved, so did the accompanying philanthropy. They also noted that new wealth would be generated by this new wave of successful businesses which could ultimately bolster the city as a whole. Rather than just writing grant cheques (which they still do), they wanted to look at an issue and find the best way for them to help address it. They realised that with their resources and networks in the nonprofit world and elsewhere they could "open up access to the new innovation, the new jobs and the new economy across LA." Cinny explained that the Annenberg Foundation "wants to make sure that we don't end up creating a sector where the wealth only stays in one part of the city, accessible to a very select few."

One of the best examples of this is Pledge LA, set up in 2018 as a joint venture with the LA venture capital community and the Mayor of Los Angeles, Eric Garcetti. The Annenberg Foundation wanted to engage the venture community with a view to improving collective impact, diversity and inclusion across organisations and investment decisions. It's a shared goal which has led to a results-driven group where all have pledged to hold themselves accountable by releasing data relating to their businesses.

By analysing the data gathered, problems can more easily be identified and programmes put in place to address the issues at hand. For example, in an inaugural survey of the venture community, only 8% of respondents identified as Latino, even though the Los Angeles' population is more than 48% Latino. This led to a programme that actively places people from under-represented backgrounds in top-tier LA-based VCs. Having diverse voices in the room, truly getting a say in who and what gets invested in, can give different perspectives. After all, this is just good business.

Talking to teams from Pledge LA, Annenberg and LA-based VCs about my social impact theory of business leaders in Los Angeles, they confirmed that there is a focus on results other than, or at least in addition to, profits. The Pledge LA survey showed that some 32% of VC firms hold investments in triple bottom line (people, profit, planet) companies, with a further 26% having this under consideration.

Summarising the thinking, Afdhel Aziz, author of 'Good is the New Cool', explained from his Silicon Beach studio that his research and countless interviews with CEOs and CMOs showed three shifts coming together to make companies need to show their social impact:

- As the Pledge LA data shows, investors have more focus on people and planet and are building it into their term sheets.
- There is a growth in consumer desire to buy from brands they believe in. People want to feel good about where they spend their money, and more access to information means that consumers now know a lot more about brands than they used to.
- Employees want to contribute to a greater good and derive meaning from their work, rather than just earning money, so a purpose-driven mission can attract more talent.

If a company can embrace these things authentically, the stats show that it reflects positively in their profits.

"For the businesses of Los Angeles, doing well is no longer the sole standard for success; so is doing good. To tap into Angelenos' spirit of activism, civic engagement, and social responsibility, the city is making common cause with the tech, entertainment, venture capital, and non-profit sectors. Major local companies are providing funding, internship opportunities, workforce development, and mentorship programs to young people from underserved communities. In turn, our rising industries are leading the charge on developing an inclusive workforce that reflects the diversity of Los Angeles. Everywhere we look, the story is the same: social impact is part of the LA zeitgeist. Everyone's bottom line is strengthened by embracing this ethic of service; and everyone is playing a role in making us the capital of creativity, culture, and a more equal and just future."

Los Angeles Mayor Eric Garcetti, Forbes, June 2018

Angelenos do it differently

One of the best things about a relatively new ecosystem, especially one anchored in the creative industries, is that there are no hard and fast rules. Where Silicon Valley has tried and tested methods for funding models and growing businesses, and Wall Street is highly structured, Los Angeles prides itself on doing things differently. It's a city of people who don't like being confined by the status quo. Which is probably why it attracts smart, creative people.

For example, Jamie Siminoff the founder of Ring, a wifi-enabled video doorbell company that started in Santa Monica in 2012, broke several Silicon Valley startup rules:

- Usually sneered at as pure entertainment and not serious by traditional VCs, Jamie went against the grain and signed up for TV show Shark Tank in 2013 to pitch his product, then called DoorBot. None of the 'sharks' invested but sales went up, generating $3 million in sales in the following months.
- Next he went on QVC, the free-to-air shopping channel, usually seen as downmarket and an unsustainable marketing channel. By 2017 he was selling millions of dollars of product on QVC alone.
- NBA legend Shaquille O'Neal (known as Shaq) loved the product, which by 2015 was called Ring. He sought CEO Jamie out and suggested he help market the product. Jamie signed Shaq up, recognising that when consumers had the choice of doorbell, they were more likely to remember the one associated with this famous sports star. Shaq also made an investment in the business and became the face of Ring.
- Jamie recognised the marketing value of being on TV, even in a non-traditional sense, and his bet paid off. In 2017 Jamie sold Ring to Amazon for $1 billion. It remains in Santa Monica and has grown its product line to become a home security company.

Photo credit: Ring

Doing business LA style

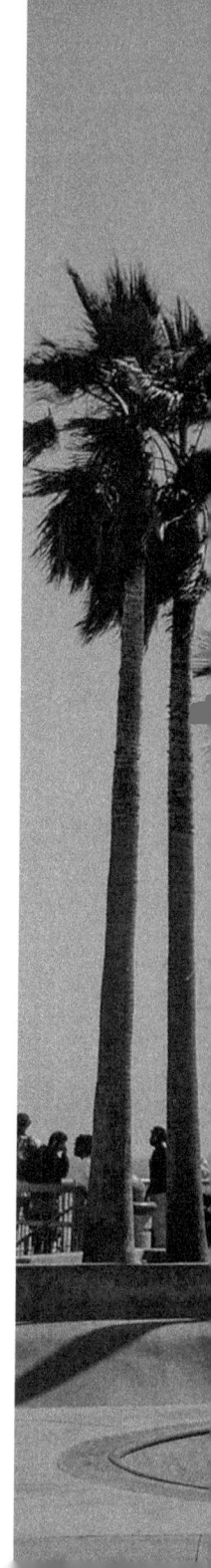

Scratch the surface and it's easy to see that much of LA's business culture stems from its Hollywood roots. In Hollywood, meetings are casual, often taking place over coffees and lunches. Big roles and scripts are not advertised - deals are done through a network of contacts which, in Hollywood, comes down to agents and managers.

An actress friend whose last role was opposite Jean-Claude van Damme couldn't get her head around how her husband, who works for a tech company, managed his own meetings. "But who figures out when to meet? And who books the restaurants for you?" she'd ask him. His daily routine of back-to-back 30-minute video conferences was a world away from hers.

In this part of the world, people don't want to miss an opportunity. So if someone comes recommended, they'll usually make time to meet. The conversation always flows but the underlying question is "Do I like you, and do you like me? Do we want to work together?". There is more emphasis in LA on personal relationships and ways of working than there is elsewhere.

It's relatively straightforward to get a first meeting through mutual contacts. Within a few months of arriving in LA, I found myself having coffee with a screenwriter who won his first Oscar two weeks later. Our conversation was lively and engaged, and so I thought the meeting had gone well. But I never heard from him again. This lack of follow-up is fairly typical: nobody in Hollywood likes to burn bridges.

The VC community isn't that different: no one wants to miss an opportunity for a follow-up funding round or the next business. So it's rare to hear 'no'; silence is far more likely. (No wonder this is where the term 'ghosting' is rumoured to have originated.)

A penchant for meeting face-to-face is entrenched in LA culture. Perhaps it's the basis of all creative industries. Your network, and

what you can bring to a meeting, is key. Face-to-face doesn't always mean coffee or lunch - for an in-depth conversation, you may be asked to go on a hike. Walking and talking without other distractions can be a great way to get to know someone and talk through an idea or problem.

There are other reasons why LA is such a face-to-face city. One theory is that executives live in big homes, drive to work and have their own offices. People are spread out, they don't live on top of each other. And because you don't have people in your personal space on the streets, on public transport and in your apartment building, you have more room to breathe and want to welcome people into your personal space.

Given Los Angeles' economic success over the last few years, those who live here want to see success around them - it's an 'all ships rise together' mentality. This city is still the underdog, and so we stick together.

This is the ultimate networking city, which suits some but not all. I love the colourful characters living and working here, their fascinating stories, the sharing of nuggets of information and exploring ways to collaborate. That, for me, is the heart of the matter. The connections which follow are the cherry on the cake. Come open to talk, explore opportunities and build from there.

Getting situated: Silicon Beach

You may have heard of Silicon Beach. Originally named as LA's answer to San Francisco's Silicon Valley, it sits on the west side of the city stretching from LAX airport to the Santa Monica Mountains. It's home to more than 500 tech startup companies and the LA HQ for tech giants such as Google, Facebook, YouTube and Yahoo.

1. YouTube Space LA
2. Facebook LA
3. Snap
4. Headspace
5. Tastemade
6. Bird.Co
7. goop Lab
8. ring
9. Dollar Shave Club
10. Vice Media
11. dosist
12. Scopely
13. SweetFlower
14. Amazon Studios
15. Universal Music Group
16. AT&T Entertainment
17. Verizon Media
18. Beats by Dre
19. Maker Studios
20. Fullscreen
21. eSalon

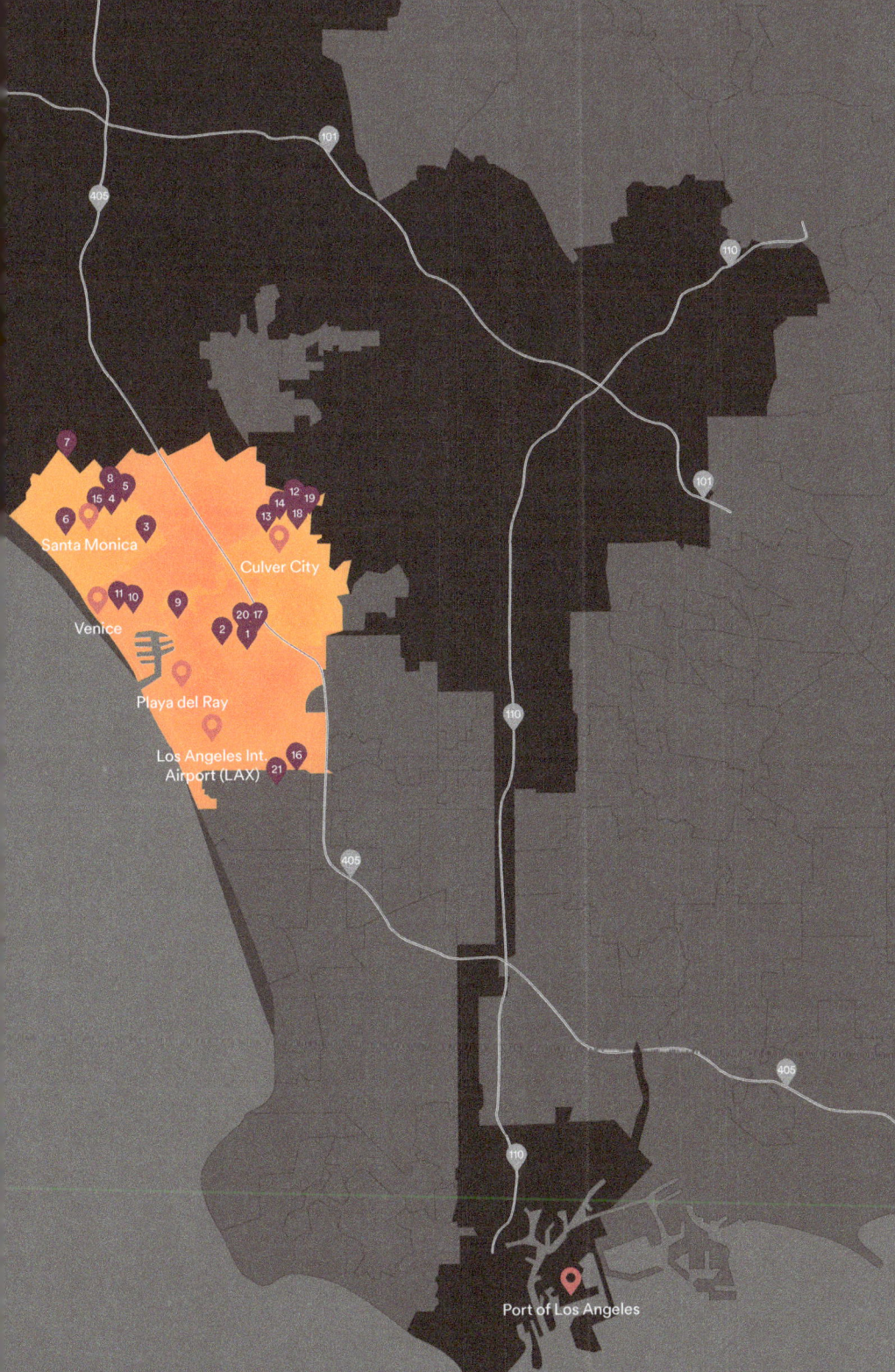

Getting situated: LA County

Silicon Beach is only a slice of the pie. There are innovative businesses across the whole of LA. And it should be noted that Angelenos are fairly loose with their definition of what constitutes their city.

LA City (shown as dark orange on the map) sits in LA County (shown as light orange on the map), alongside 87 other independent municipalities, all with their own mayor and city council. These other municipalities are often cities regarded as part of LA; they're not LA City but they do fall within LA County. They include Santa Monica, Beverly Hills and West Hollywood (not Hollywood or the Hollywood Hills which are both part of LA City). In short, it's complicated. Just know that 'LA' could mean pretty much anywhere in the vicinity.

1. SpaceX
2. Riot Games Inc.
3. Hyperloop One
4. The Honest Company
5. Kitchen United Pasadena
6. Cloud Kitchens
7. Technicolor Experience Center
8. Next Heath
9. NASA Jet Propulsion Labratory
10. Los Angeles Cleantech Incubator
11. GTs Living Foods
12. Netflix
13. Homeboy Industries
14. Soylent Innovation Lab
15. MedMen
16. Sweetgreen
17. Sony Pictures Studios
18. Walt Disney Studios
19. Warner Bros. Studios
20. Universal Studios Hollywood
21. Honey
22. Google 'Spruce Goose'
23. BCG Digital Ventures
24. Northrop Grumman Aerospace Systems
25. TOMS Shoes

Media, Entertainment & Music

Media, entertainment and music

Ask people what first comes to mind at the mention of Los Angeles and they'll say the entertainment industry, aka Hollywood. In reality – and this will surprise many – entertainment is only the city's third largest industry.

True, it is one of LA's oldest industries, dating back to the early 20th century. The origins of some of the city's booming contemporary industries can be traced right back to Hollywood – besides which, it adds a level of glam that other cities just don't have.

The talent is here, the business is done here, and so are pre- and post-editing. The filming now mostly takes place elsewhere though, since that's usually a cheaper option. This hasn't always been the case however, and the city has provided a backdrop for many of the world's biggest movies.

'Talent' is what Hollywood calls celebrities. The rest of us mere mortals may be talented at other things, but acting is king in Hollywood. In LA you quickly get used to rubbing shoulders with celebrities, whether it's Tom Hanks sitting behind you in a restaurant looking fresh as a daisy after a trip with Obama, or Natalie Portman eating a salad in a cafe with her baby beside her. On more than one occasion when I was hosting a round-table discussion as background for this book, I spotted Arnold Schwarzenegger. Either it turns out he likes breakfast at the Fairmont too, or else he is following me around town.

Media, Entertainment & Music

The studio lots are significant in this city, always filled with tourists in summer from the theme parks of Disney and Universal to the studio tours of Warner Bros, Paramount and Sony. I confess that I love taking meetings on the lots and catching a glimpse of a new TV show or movie being made. There's just something magical about it.

Dear Hollywood, you've changed!

Los Angeles-based author and Vanity Fair correspondent Nick Bilton says: "Hollywood as we know it is already over." He offers convincing arguments about long, complicated processes and a costly unionised workforce, though his is very much the dystopian view.

It is true that Hollywood has been shaken to its core over the last few years, mostly thanks to the huge success of disruptive streaming companies such as Netflix. This has also caused consolidation in the market, most recently with Disney buying Fox. Now there are just four traditional Hollywood studios remaining: Disney, Warner, Universal and Sony. Competition is coming from new entrants to the market which include Netflix, Amazon, Hulu and, soon, Apple.

According to the Hollywood Reporter, North American box office sales hit an all-time high in 2018, increasing by 7% to $11.9 billion. Movie-going is still popular – but how that happens is what's changed for studios. They used to enjoy big cinematic showings with long releases often lasting for months before rental release and home purchase. Now Netflix and co are releasing films for a limited time to cinemas (mostly for award qualification purposes) or streaming straight into people's homes.

Similarly, while viewers had to wait for an exact time on a certain day of every week for their favourite TV show to air, now whole series are 'dropped' for us to watch as and when we please. We want it and we want it now. Welcome to the world of binge watching.

And so the definition of 'movies' is changing: does it matter if we watch a 180-minute movie or six 30-minute episodes? The decision is based on the best format for the content itself, not on how it is produced. As a result, we're hearing a lot about the 'golden age of TV'. The quality is good and there's an ambition for new series to attract a lot of attention. What better way to do that than by employing high-profile movie stars? First came House of Cards with Kevin Spacey, then more and more A-list actors migrated to the small screen, among them Julia Roberts, Meryl Streep, Nicole Kidman, Penelope Cruz, Colin Farrell, Amy Adams, Reese Witherspoon and Benedict Cumberbatch. The list goes on.

Thinking about content in a holistic way rather than by release type - cinematic, scripted, non-scripted - has prepared the studios to launch their own streaming services (Disney+, Warner Media) to compete with Netflix. The decision to launch their own services is partly an economic one to generate revenue, partly an opportunity to have a direct relationship with their customers rather than giving this to third parties such as Netflix, Amazon, Hulu and other streaming services.

With more entrants to the market, more content is being produced which can clearly be seen from the graph below showing the estimated number of scripted original series from 2002 to 2018. One industry expert suggested that this equates to more than $20 billion dollars of additional annual revenue.

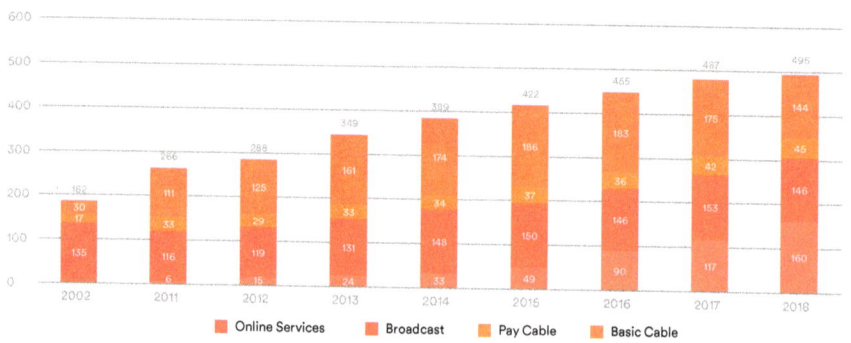

Estimated Number of Scripted Original Series in Broadcast, Cable, and Online Services

Chart source: FX Networks Research, Analysis by Beacon Economics

Technology is supporting this vast new stream of content with smoother live streaming and creators collaborating on content in the cloud in real time. Artificial Intelligence (AI) and machine learning create efficiencies which are useful in a highly-unionised industry. Technical processes such as rendering will soon be done in real time, instead of taking days. Perhaps most importantly, with online viewing becoming increasingly popular, more data is available to studios allowing them direct connections to, and feedback from, their audience about their viewing habits.

Photo credit: Ryot 5G studio

Technology will also allow more personalised content. For example, one layer of a movie could be all the written language in it such as signposts, book covers or shop names, which could easily be switched into different languages for different regions using CGI technology. |Now the content is 'glued' together so movies can be subtitled or dubbed, but the visual cues remain the same. Equally, scenes could be graded based on age suitability so that more family-friendly versions of a movie (taking out certain violent or bloody scenes, for example) could be shown, depending on who is in the room.

For advertisers, new technology could allow for much better audience targeting (which has only been feasible online and has been a huge contributor to the success of social networks). In my version of the film I may see bottles of sparkling water, while my father may see beer brands in his version.

Technically, studios can also offer more 'choose your own adventure' content such as Steven Soderburgh's Mosaic or Netflix's Bandersnatch. These are lean-forward participatory experiences rather than the usual relaxed lean-back form of a film, a format where a creative expert has already taken all the decisions to give you the best experience. As a senior Disney executive told me: "decisions can't be fully data-driven in such a creative industry, they will be data-informed".

What will we see in futuro? Will we have mini-projectors turning the walls of our ounge into a cinema? Or will all movies be in 3D, viewed via headsets? Will we watch movies in our self-driving cars? Or will we continue to be glued to our small-screen mobile phones? These are all questions that studio innovation labs are asking, and for which they areseeking solutions.

The new celebrities taking over the media world

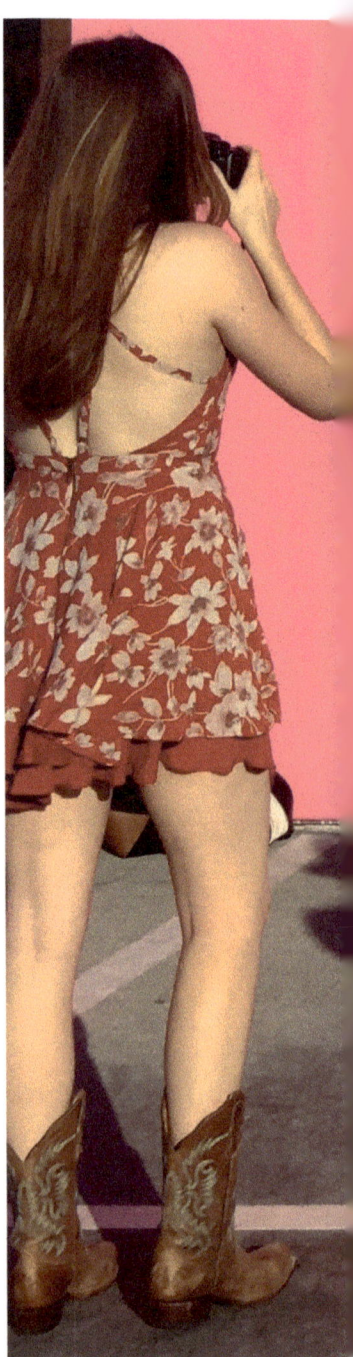

The definition of entertainment is changing. 'Entertainment' now encompasses every app and form of media available via a phone. After all, these are things you take time to look at, and it's your time that entertainment companies are competing for. Hence the term 'attention economy'. Generations are growing up without focusing on one thing at a time.

Nielsen research in 2018[1] shows that 45% of people in the US use a digital device like a phone or tablet while watching TV. Only 12% say they never use a digital device when watching television.

Why is this? Digital video platforms such as YouTube and TikTok, and social media platforms from Facebook to Snapchat, are creating viable alternatives to traditional TV. Gen Z is the first fully digital native generation, most of them 'cable nevers' (they've never subscribed to cable TV).

As everyone now has a smartphone in their pocket, they are also able to create content. James Creech, Co-Founder & CEO of Paladin, which provides influencer marketing software to agencies and media companies globally, explains:

"As technology democratized access to content creation and consumption, millions of people all over the world have embraced the creator moniker, particularly young people."

He goes on to explain how this gave rise to a new class of online entertainers, such as vloggers (video bloggers), gamers (creators who live stream themselves playing video games), make-up tutorialists,

[1] Techcrunch 2018 'Nielsen: the second screen is booming as 45% often or always use devices while watching TV'

Photo credit: Lippe Oosterhof

unboxers (who unveil new products by literally opening the box onscreen), and other online personalities, collectively known as social influencers. This new creator class is building loyal audiences that rival, and in some cases eclipse, those of traditional media outlets.

With these new categories of entertainers, the definition of the celebrity A-list is changing. Online gaming sensation PewDiePie, who you may or may not have heard of, boasts 101 million subscribers to his YouTube channel. That's comparable to the Super Bowl, arguably the biggest sporting event in the U.S., which drew 98.2 million television viewers in 2019! Crazy numbers, right?

While social media platforms offered a place for creators all over the world to generate loyal followings, Los Angeles has been the natural hub for the new business of social media influencers. LA already has the infrastructure in place to manage traditional entertainment businesses, and these new stars aren't that different. To help influencers make the most of the LA network and maximise their brands as businesses, management companies such as Maker Studios and Fullscreen emerged. Both of these companies were snapped up by traditional entertainment studios and larger content companies looking to understand and embrace these new stars (Disney bought Maker in 2014, and Fullscreen is now owned by Otter Media, a subsidiary of AT&T's Warner Media).

James explains: "Today LA's gravitational pull has grown stronger, inspiring international creators like Lilly Singh and Lele Pons to relocate to the world's largest media market. Despite the fact that technology has enabled influencers to create from anywhere, they're choosing to be in LA because of the access and career opportunities it provides."

It's also true that traditional celebrities are embracing social media to connect with fans. The Digital Marketing Institute put singer Selena Gomez and football Cristiano Ronaldo in their Top Ten social media influencer rankings for 2019. With so many changes, what constitutes a 'celebrity' changes for different generations and different demographics. When I speak to teenagers visiting LA, they are more interested in the YouTube Studios and SnapChat than in visiting the traditional Hollywood Stars Walk of Fame. Perhaps in time lines will blur, but for now different screens and platforms create celebrities for different audiences. Either way, Los Angeles seems set to remain at the epicentre of the global media revolution.

Mobile is the new TV: how habits are changing

In the US, cable cutting is rife. Expensive cable subscriptions, known as bundles, are being dumped in favour of subscription platforms like Hulu, Netflix and Amazon. Consumers can still stream on their TV, but most prefer to do so on their computer, tablet or phone. The concept of staying in at a particular time on a particular evening to watch a desired show is anathema.

As technology develops, more services are moving to the cloud, and the promise of greater connectivity offered by 5G means a better viewing experience for people on the move. Mobile has become the most popular device for digital media in terms of time spent each day.

With its proximity to Silicon Valley and the hard shift in TV viewing to streaming on digital devices, Hollywood understands the changing digital landscape only too well. With this in mind, Los Angeles is embracing change and the buzz is all about the mobile platform.

Here are some of the exciting LA-based companies embracing the (very) small screen:

Quibi

Perhaps the most notable example is Jeffrey Katzenberg and Meg Whitman's Quibi. Based in Los Angeles, they are bringing Silicon Valley tech and entertainment know-how into one platform for 'quick bites'. They will be spending $1 billion on content between now and 2025 and are ramping up quickly. The idea behind this is simple. Most TV viewing is made up of one-hour segments: they are looking to provide a platform where compelling content is made for a 10-minute segment and is easily found. Whitman notes that it takes a user an average of eight minutes to find content on Netflix, which is too long for mobile.

Many of the big Hollywood studios are on board, as well as notable celebrities like actor Leonardo DiCaprio and director Guillermo del Toro. This isn't a new platform of short-form video; it's high-quality production (think HBO) but in shorter segments (60 or 90 minutes), designed to be watched in 10-minute segments. Although the launch date hasn't been confirmed, it's likely to be late 2019 or early 2020.

Mammoth Media

Based in Santa Monica, Mammoth Media has been experimenting with storytelling in different formats such as Yarn, which tells stories through text conversations. They call it a 'chat fiction app', with stories told across a number of genres such as romance, mystery, thriller and horror. By owning the IP and the delivery, through their own apps they can also focus on monetisation, working directly with brands on sponsorships.

To give some context to this, they say that 60 million stories and eight billion messages have been read to date, and that the average user reads four times per day for two minutes per session, totalling 56 minutes in their first week. Those are impressive stats.

Snap

There cannot be a discussion about mobile video without discussing Snap. While Snap has its problems, in the second quarter of 2019 it attracted 203 million daily active users - which is 80 million more than Twitter. Snap has been innovative in creating different formats for mobile and has been a pioneer of vertical video with split screens, text over video and motion graphics.

These platforms are not built on flash-in-the-pan ideas tossed out into the world to see if they can garner a viral hit - they are well thought out, data-driven organisations. We're going to see more exciting new ways to tell stories over mobile in the coming years.

How LA became the global hub for sweet sweet music

Traditionally the music industry was based where the decision-makers were for broadcasters, radio and advertisers, which was, and mostly still is, in New York. As the world became more digital, music was more prevalent on platforms outside traditional broadcast such as Spotify, YouTube and Apple Music, and much of the advertising became automated through programmatic platforms where fewer direct relationships were needed. This all meant less reliance on New York but no real need to change.

There are several theories about how and why LA became the greater hub - partly for the reasons described above, but there is always a catalyst. Rumour has it that a single person was the catalyst for this change. The Head of Universal Music Group moved from London to NY. He bought a house in Connecticut and did a trial commute for a week. He hated it so much that he sold the house and moved to sunny LA instead.

There are many sound reasons for the music industry to be in Los Angeles. It's the home of Hollywood, many artists live in LA, and the predominant touring companies (AEG and Livenation) and talent agents (CAA etc) are much closer to the tech platforms in Silicon Valley.

Technology is changing the music industry.

These three startups are among the many which are transforming the face of music:

Music rights management

Malibu-based Orfium uses AI to recognise when proprietary music is played across user generated content (UGC) platforms such as YouTube and Facebook. It effectively collects royalties on music that has been played without consent – something which has long been a thorn in the music labels' side. Through this they have been able to automate rights management, royalties and reporting for major music companies, and help artists expand their digital distribution and global rights management.

Photo credit: crbellette / Shutterstock.com

Music creation

Out of music accelerator Techstars in Los Angeles comes data and AI-led Endel, which creates 'personalised sounds to help you focus, relax, and sleep'. Endel takes in data such as the time of day, local weather and your calendar to see how busy you are, to create personal soundscapes. They have musicians on staff who create the stems of the tracks. These are then adapted via AI technology using the science of circadian rhythms, layering in sound masking to create sounds that are harmonious to the brain to help you either focus, relax or sleep.

Endel claims a 6.3x increase in concentration and a 3.6% decrease in anxiety when people listen to their tracks - impressive numbers. Now that sophisticated AI systems can create songs without artists, is the definition of artists changing?

Music distribution and payments

Digital music platforms have proliferated and the cost of production and distribution has dropped, allowing more artists to go direct to consumers. Artists often know how to market their music but each platform has different models, making the administrative burden a heavy one. West Hollywood-based Stem is a platform that helps creators build their business through software as a service (SAAS) platform. The company treats artists as entrepreneurs, and sees itself as the COO to execute the vision and build the business. This is probably the first time there has been easy transparency in a busy industry of artists, songwriters, producers, managers, labels and platforms. Will this be a growing business as more independent artists break out of the old hierarchical system?

Will.i.am's
hi-tech approach

Will.i.am has quite a presence in Los Angeles. His office, which houses teams for all his projects from studios to I.AM+ speech technology Omega and from 'button' headphones to fashion, is called The Future. Not far from the Paramount movie lot, it's an innocuous building from the outside. However inside, after you've gone through the secure lobby and signed your life away in a Non-Disclosure Agreement, it's all white lines, geometric shapes and two green-screen fully-soundproofed studios. As we get the tour, we see a full wardrobe van out the back, bursting at the seams with Will's fashion choices. There's also a custom-built Tesla in the car park.

Given Will.i.am's entrepreneurial spirit, it's no wonder the Black Eyed Peas are experimenting with new technology to enhance the experience of their concert-goers. For their Master of the Sun tour, they created an AR app with Santa Monica-based Trigger - The Mixed Reality Agency™

With prompts from the band at certain songs, the app allowed users to interact with the music. At most concerts you see the audience using their phones to shoot photos and video: adding an AR experience isn't changing user behaviour, it's augmenting it. The 30-50% of the audience who downloaded the app enjoyed extra treats: for the song Big Love, for example, they could swipe up to send hearts which built into a big heart, and for I Gotta Feeling, a virtual spaceship hovered over the stage playing a light show.

It's likely we will be seeing more of this as apps can be developed to add other features that benefit on-site users such as automated ticket checks, credit for concessions and merchandise (mobile payments), as well as ordering drinks in advance to skip the queues.

Hollywood's fun new toy

There has been much hype around virtual reality. Some disappointment too - headsets are still clunky and fairly expensive and it's generally a solo experience - but Hollywood has found ways to bring VR to story making, such as in 2019's film The Lion King, and story viewing with in-person consumer experiences.

Chantal Rickards, CEO of the British Academy of Film and Television Arts (BAFTA) in Los Angeles, sees a future bursting with immersive technology. "With VR we have found a device, a concept and an art form all rolled into one, which is on the cutting edge of technology yet pushes emotional boundaries in vital and visceral ways. VR may have had a hiccup or two along the way, but anyone who saw the VR exhibition at LACMA by [Oscar winning Director] Alejandro Inarritu of the extraordinary Carne y Arena will have been left in no doubt about the power of VR to persuade, cajole, move, mesmerise and shock."

Premiered at the Cannes Film Festival in 2017, this was a thrilling piece of filmmaking. No spoilers here - see it if you get the opportunity.

There is also Santa Monica-based Dreamscape which offers fun experiences akin to a virtual Jurassic Park, Indiana Jones or underwater adventure. Its creators hail from impressive Hollywood backgrounds including Disney, and one of the co-founders was the first to receive an Emmy award for interactive content. These experiences take you into other worlds and have wowed everyone I have taken there. Dreamscape offers 20-minute location-based experiences in groups of six. In Westfield Century City their space sits opposite the cinema, also an investor in Dreamscape. It's easy to see that this could be the future of movies.

New technologies also allow for more experimentation and deeper experiences, not only for consumers but also for creators. Most studios now have volumetric stages. These are large green screen rooms with multiple cameras to capture action in 3D. Rather than choosing from three or four camera angles, a director can choose from hundreds of them. Sony Entertainment has used this method to create a virtual set for the popular 'Shark Tank' TV show, enabling much more flexibility in their interviews.

Locations can be captured through multiple photos 'stitched' together to create 3D versions, known as photogrammetry. A camera can capture a whole room in minutes. Rather than send people out location scouting for days on end, a drone can take this footage and be back with a 3D image in a matter of hours. At the Disney StudioLAB you can see this in action, with one location meant to be a rudimentary model, created for scouting purposes, being manipulated to feature in the intro to a Marvel movie.

In 2019, Disney's The Lion King was filmed using a volumetric studio and computer generated graphics (CGI). This in itself is unique, but one of the things that really struck me is how Disney Innovation Lab spent some time adapting old-school movie-making equipment for use in 3D so that top filmmakers could seamlessly transition to shooting in this new way. For example, a traditional camera dolly was linked to the virtual game engine software in which the movie was being made so that the cameraman and director could produce smooth, sweeping shots rather than have to use a VR hand controller. Another camera simply had one of the VR hand controllers attached on top of a normal camera so that they could get the feel of traditional camera angles. Aside from allowing traditional talent to adapt easily to new mediums, it gives viewers the same camera shots and movements they are used to.

Once built in 3D, the assets can easily be adapted for use in other environments such as computer games, social media or even holograms.

Chantal Rickards, CEO BAFTA LA, sums up the use of VR in Hollywood:

"I don't yet fear that technology will subjugate human creativity. We will always need our Shakespeares and our Spielbergs. We will always be appreciative of the human brain power that goes into telling a wonderful story and we will always want to tell each other stories; it's how we communicate, it is relatable, it brings down walls and democratises our world."

Celebrity: the strange new reality

Photo credit: Instagram, @lilmiquela

As we've seen with the evolution of new platforms and technologies, the definition of celebrity is changing. Take Lil Miquela, a 19 year-old Angeleno who is prolific on Instagram where she has 1.6 million followers. Many of her posts are focused in and around Los Angeles featuring streetwear, palm trees and local landmarks. She's often found with her two best friends, Bermuda and Blawko, also Angelenos. With a growing following, Lil Miquela has been doing some powerful endorsements, working with fashion companies such as Chanel and Kenzo, as well as partnering with YouTube at Coachella 2019 to interview musicians.

What's so exciting about this? When you look at Lil Miquela's account, you may notice something slightly off with her. I couldn't quite work it out to start with. She's almost perfect but looks enhanced in some way - and that's because Lil Miquela isn't real. She's a virtual influencer, created by Los Angeles-based Brud. This fact was announced by Bermuda, Lil Miquela's 'friend', who 'hacked' her account, telling Lil Miquela's followers that she wasn't being true to them and should confess.

Now she (or should I say 'it'?) is quite open about being a robot, and people don't seem to care. In fact, this plays well. It makes her different and several ad campaigns are featuring her.

This technology is fascinating but Brud isn't the only company using it; they've just been smart in execution, raising awareness and, in turn, securing funding.

The level of realism is improving all the time. After all, this is an iteration of 3D modelling. Scanning technologies from specialist and major technology providers such as Microsoft and Metastage allow humans to be scanned and placed in VR and AR environments. Combine this with Artificial Intelligence (AI) and the use of Computer Generated Images (CGI) - there are myriad experts in Los Angeles who come from world-building for pre-visualisation in movies - and you'll see that these digital humans can be animated for use in new digital worlds.

It's now relatively easy to take 3D video of human forms which can be used for a number of digital purposes. The mobile app Holo, by 8i, was one of the early ones allowing consumers to place 'digital humans' in videos with themselves using AR. Influencers have jumped on board, so fans can now take virtual selfies and virtual videos with their favourite influencer.

Many celebrities in Los Angeles have outsourced their social media to specialists in the field. So will they soon be including their digital likeness? Does the celeb need to actually be there to endorse a product - or could their digital likeness be adapted for photoshoots? After all a celebrity is a brand, just like Lil Miquela.

Photo credit: Instagram, @lilmiquela

TL;DR

- Hollywood is where the business is - agents, talent and post-production are all here, even if filming is done elsewhere to cut costs.

- There is a proliferation of content - more platforms across more devices means more is being made.

- Hollywood is where the music is - the industry has shifted from New York to be closer to artists, agents and platforms.

- Mobile-specific content is still in its infancy but has high visibility, with top Hollywood talent committing to Jeffrey Katzenberg's Quibi and prominent brands creating shows on Snap.

- The definition of celebrity is changing alongside the growth of new platforms such as YouTube, Snapchat and now TikTok.

- More technology gives filmmakers more tools to create content and establish direct relationships with their audiences.

- New technology is allowing different types of content creation, immersing people in a 3D world with Virtual Reality.

- Digital 'characters' will become more realistic, making it tough to differentiate between 'real' and 'fake' humans.

An inspiring story of innovation: rethinking charity

Matt Pohlson sits in Omaze's trendy warehouse office space surrounded by images of happy people standing next to and laughing with celebrities including George Clooney, Jennifer Lawrence, Channing Tatum, John Legend and many more. All these celebrities have taken part in an Omaze campaign which raised hundreds of thousands - if not millions - of dollars for charity. But Omaze isn't a non-profit organisation.

To understand how it got to where it is today, we have to go back a decade.

When Matt was at Wharton Business School doing an MBA in 2008/2009, he made some new friends. The group of people at the business school was special. Perhaps it was because it was a tough year to get into the MBA following the Wall Street crash and subsequent recession; perhaps it was all down to a particularly inspirational teacher. Either way, there is a riveting documentary waiting to be made about this one group of friends who left college to launch some of today's most successful businesses, all of them with a social impact element: AllBirds, Warby Parker, Lola, Beyond Meat and Omaze, to name a few.

Their success has created a rock-solid support network between these first-time entrepreneurs.

It was at Wharton that Matt met his co-founder, Ryan Cummins. Shortly after the MBA programme they were back in LA and invited at the last minute to a glitzy black tie fundraising event.

Photo credit: Omaze

Matt explains that they were often drafted in last minute to fill seats, despite not being wealthy donors, they scrubbed up well for these events.

On this particular evening, they left the gala both heartbroken and inspired. There had been an auction item to shoot hoops with their childhood hero, basketball player Magic Johnson, yet they were quickly outbid and couldn't nearly reach the $15,000 it would have taken to win, especially with debts from their MBA.

Why were these types of opportunities only available for the wealthy? On the way home they talked about ways in which these kinds of auctions could be democratised so the general public could attend, while still creating revenue for charity. Their conversation also turned to the film 'The Inconvenient Truth' by Al Gore, which had created a lot of awareness but had little lasting impact.

By combining these two models - working with high-profile celebrities and using storytelling techniques to talk about issues - they believed they could create donation-based campaigns to raise funds and awareness for charities. In addition, this could open up a whole new donation model for charities.

Anyone can enter their campaigns - the more money donated to charity, the more entries a person will receive. By working with high-profile celebrities and charities, they can leverage audiences across platforms to reach more people.

Matt and Ryan aren't fans of the traditional non-profit model as they thought they'd be stuck in constant fundraising cycles to operate the business and create sufficient funds for marketing. Instead, they manage these campaigns on behalf of the charity - investing in the technology, marketing, legal, and fulfillment aspects that are often out of reach for nonprofits - and take a percentage of the proceeds. This for-profit model has allowed Omaze to grow into the 105 person team it is today, leading their own initiatives such as working with Los Angeles Unified School District (LAUSD) to help bring meditation and optimism centers to middle schools (a very LA initiative!).

The business has generated over $200 million for charities including Comic Relief, Slow Food, United Nations Foundation, Malala Fund, The Clooney Foundation for Justice, and many more.

Matt tells me the story of having to cancel a meeting scheduled with Pope Francis (yes, the Pope Francis). A business is fairly special if it manages to secure an audience with the Pope, particularly with a view to taking part in a campaign, but Matt had good reason to cancel. Technically, he died.

One day Matt suddenly felt terribly ill and went to the hospital. Omaze's COO, Helen Melluish met him there. After some initial exams the doctors weren't sure what was wrong so they sent Helen home to get some rest and said they would look after Matt until she returned in the morning.

Photo credit: Omaze

> "I was grateful for what I had accomplished, but also impatient for what I hadn't yet done."

However when Helen got home she had a bad feeling, so she turned her car around and went back to the hospital. As she arrived, Matt's heart rate started to crash. He was rushed into surgery where they discovered some scar tissue from a stomach problem he was born with had become loose and created an obstruction.

They removed the scar tissue but Matt's heart rate didn't recover. In fact it got worse. By this time his parents and brother were also at the hospital. They heard a call for Code Blue in Matt's room, which his mother, a nurse, recognised: he was flatlining. She managed to talk her way into the room and saw a team using resuscitation paddles to try to bring her son back to life.

After a couple of minutes they were going to give up but his mum turned around to see many faces at the window. The nurses had all gathered, and seeing them inspired Matt's mum to tell him not to give up and to try harder. She persuaded them to keep trying. Then, four minutes into flatlining, the doctor noticed a pulse, Matt suddenly raised his hand and gave the thumbs up.

Technically he had been dead, and there was no specific medical reason for him to be alive today with his full faculties.

As you can imagine, 'dying' - even for a few minutes - changes your perspective. Matt said he emerged from this experience feeling much more optimistic. One of the impacts for Omaze was Matt's realisation that the core attraction of its consumer offering was the experience itself. Sometimes this was the opportunity to take home a Ferrari instead of a date night out with a celebrity. As a result, Omaze has started creating more dream experiences and this, in turn, has raised more for charities. Their new goal is to be the first for-profit company to raise $1 billion for charity in a single year. And somehow I think they'll manage it.

Gaming

LA's got game

Photo credit: Riot Games

Have you ever played Candy Crush on your phone? Chances are, you have. Along with 270 million other people. Yes, that's 270 million - about 60 million more than the combined populations of the UK, France and Germany. That's a lot of people.

What about League of Legends? No? Have you heard of it? This is a much more involved game and is played by more than 80 million people per month. That's about 16 million more people than the UK population, or double the population of the most densely populated state in the US: (yes, California).

These are enormous numbers by anyone's standards. Gaming as a category touches a lot more people than I realised before arriving in Los Angeles. From casual gamers who may play the occasional game on their phones or on Facebook, through to professional gamers who play the likes of League of Legends for a (well-paid) living.

This is a field with mass appeal. It's visual, it's interactive and the biggest games have incredible storylines and depth. Sounds a little like the movie business. And that's one of the reasons why gaming roots are deep in Los Angeles.

This huge span of audience means gaming has some big numbers around it and is growing. newszoo estimates that the market is worth almost $150 billion in 2019 and will grow to $174 billion by 2021.

Gaming is often misconstrued as a young male pastime. In fact 46% of gamers are female[1], the average male gamer is 33-years-old and the average female gamer is 37-years-old[2].

Age/gender of gamers

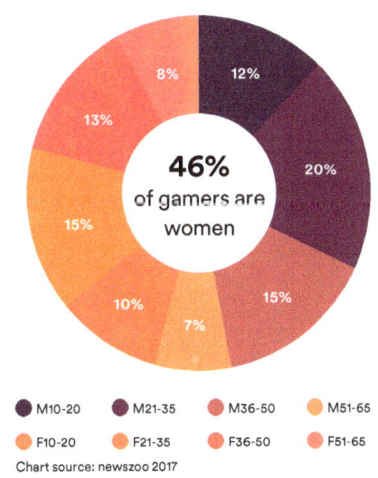

46% of gamers are women

12%
20%
15%
7%
10%
15%
13%
8%

● M10-20   ● M21-35   ● M36-50   ● M51-65
● F10-20   ● F21-35   ● F36-50   ● F51-65

Chart source: newszoo 2017

[1] newszoo, 2017. [2] The Entertainment Software Association, 2018.

Gaming and Hollywood

Many an Uber driver I've ridden with are temping 'between roles', and restaurants often have ridiculously good-looking waiters, most of whom are trying to break into the industry.

But Hollywood doesn't just need actors to succeed; there are many different talent pools that go into making blockbuster movies. Think about the CGI (computer-generated imagery) that goes into movies such as such as Avatar, Finding Nemo, Toy Story or Game of Thrones (spoiler: those dragons weren't real). All of these productions have had entire worlds created especially for them. Even those movies that don't contain CGI intrinsically often use it to pre-visualise complicated scenes (think of it as advanced storyboarding using digital techniques). And therein lies the first natural fit with gaming: each game creates its own world and has its own story, just like a Hollywood story.

Other elements needed for a great game include sound effects, music, technology and content - all of which overlap with the talent pool already serving Hollywood. Some people told me they preferred working in gaming as it allows them to be more creative. This may also explain the rise in the use of psychedelics in California - but that's a different story.

The proximity to movie studios is a benefit too. The studios make movies which become their own brands, especially with the recent spate of

action-adventure films (The Avengers, Spiderman) and animated movies (Toy Story, Finding Nemo, The Lion King). Turning these brands into games makes sense for all involved - they already have audiences that want to engage more, and what better way than by allowing them to control the characters directly? Gaming is in many ways a brand extension of Hollywood.

This has also given way to a level of serendipity in Los Angeles that shouldn't be underestimated. There is a natural level of cross collaboration that we see where relationships have started out by chance. Maybe it turns out that your roommate's brother is a script editor who noticed a famous lead actor playing your game between scenes. With a gentle nudge he posts on Instagram, which in turn gets shared and shoots this new game to fame. Stranger things have happened.

Photo credit: Section Studios

"I think it's the appetite for creativity that allows these things. People listen to the actual work. It's not that you're just the e-commerce guy and I'm a game guy, there's no natural connection between us, we're two different industries. Yet we were able to just come together and just naturally organically emerge from it."

Jimmy Yun, Section Studios, talking about the start of his collaboration with Eric Koch, That Game Company.

Gaming: a brief history

1972 — Atari was launched influencing both in-home and arcade gaming, especially with 'Pong'

1980 — Nintendo launch handheld games with Donkey Kong launched in 1982

1982 — Commodore 64 was launched

1983 — Video game crash as cartridge sales flooded the market

1985 — Super Mario Bros was launched by Nintendo

1989 — Nintendo launched Game Boy

1991 — Sega found huge success with Sonic the Hedgehog

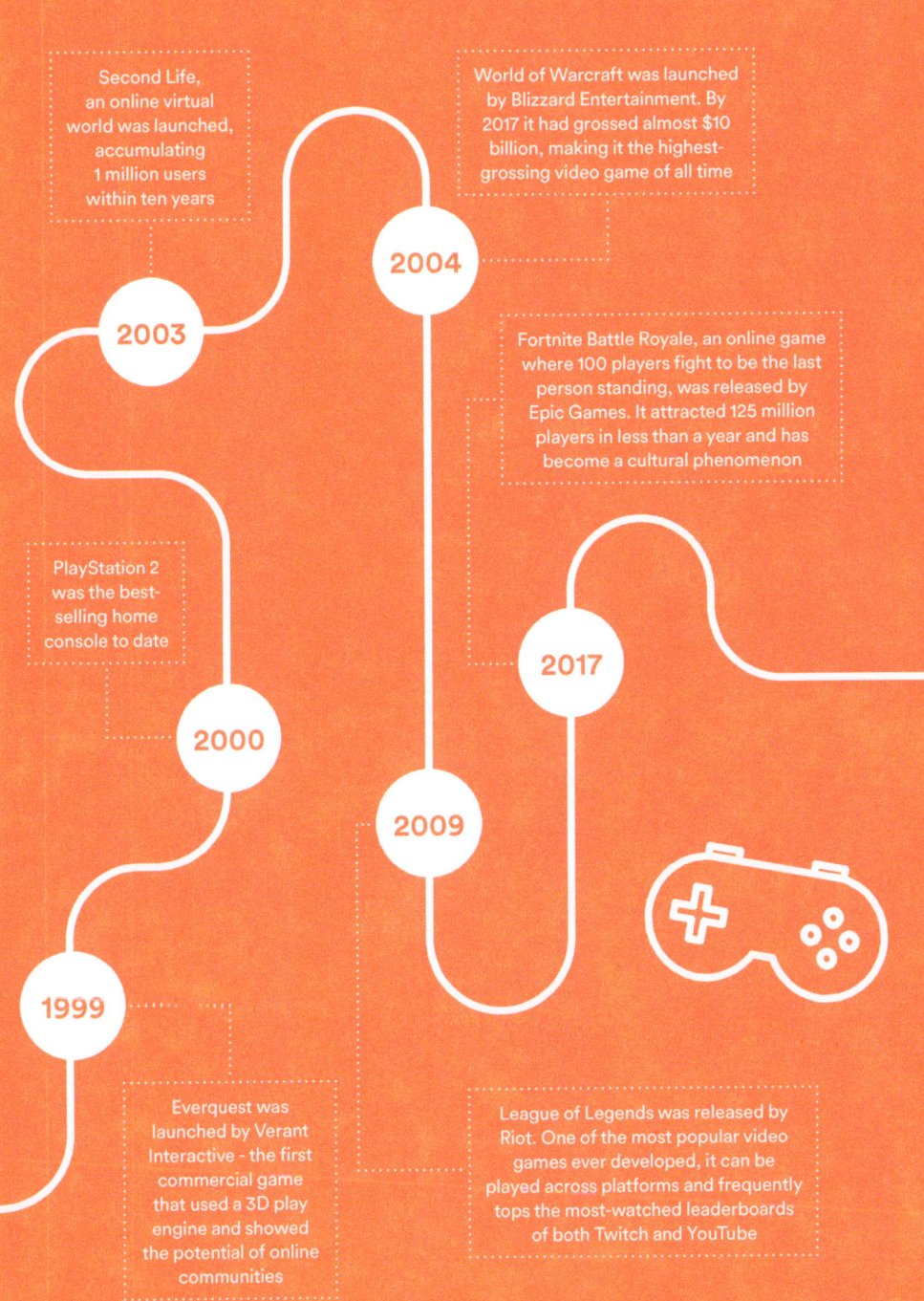

Gaming is perhaps the first industry that has nascently been split between Silicon Valley and Los Angeles. Much of the deep tech and hardware sit in Silicon Valley, as does one of the main professional conferences, GDC (Games Developer Conference), which attracts 29,000 people. The creative storytelling, game development and publishing sit in Los Angeles, along with the E3 conference which, in true LA style, is open to all and attracts 66,000 people.

Gaming is much bigger than is often perceived. To give some perspective:

There are more than **2.5bn** video gamers worldwide[3]

64% of the general US population are gamers[4]

The video games market is expected to be worth more than **$160bn** by 2020, from nearly $78.61 billion in 2017[5]

[3] The European Mobile Game Market, 2016. [4] Nielsen, 2017. [5] BestTheNews, 2016.

Gaming 101: sound like you know what you're talking about

Video game

A game played by electronically manipulating images produced by a computer programme on a monitor or other display.

This is a catch-all for gaming, a term that should only be used if you need to differentiate from an old-fashioned board game, or if you want to date yourself.

AAA (pronounced as 'triple A')

Video games produced by major publishers that have higher development and marketing budgets and are therefore expected to be of high quality.

Triple A is to gaming what blockbuster is to movies. Triple A games include God of War, Grand Theft Auto and Assassins Creed.

Console

A small electronic device for playing computerised video games.

Consoles are specialist equipment for gaming that often have accessories such as controllers (a joystick to you and me). Major brands include Sony PlayStation, Xbox and Nintendo.

PC game

A video game played on a personal computer rather than a dedicated console. They generally have higher input, processing and video output.

Many people will say that this is a declining market, but they are wrong. PC games hold firm at 10% of the market even as it grows. They are often profitable as PC games have a higher upfront cost.

Mobile game

A game played on a smartphone, tablet or smartwatch.

Unsurprisingly this is the largest market within gaming due to its huge user base, and 50% of people with a smartphone play games. Fun fact: the earliest known game was Tetris.

Here's a little more depth so you *really* sound like you know what you're talking about:

With a small screen and fewer player movement capabilities, development costs on mobile are often not as high as AAA games. However the life cycle is shorter and monetisation strategies aren't always obvious.

At the other end of the scale are PC games, which are known for their high-end capabilities and excellent graphics. While PC has shown small decline as a percentage of the overall gaming industry, numbers continue to rise which means that sector is still expanding.

Matt Calder at ESDF Management says PC games are incredibly attractive. Although they can cost more to develop (often $2-$10 million), PC gamers are loyal and are more inclined to spend more money to get the full game upfront. Successful PC gamers are also more likely to stick around for decades, rather than short-term hits.

Consoles also deliver high-end processing power, and alongside PCs attract a more dedicated gamer who wants the precision and control over the game that a controller can give over a touchscreen. Although consoles can cost less, they have a more focused use around entertainment. Consoles often sit in a different part of the house than PCs and can be shared between family members. The phrase 'battle for the living room' stems from console use and is only being amplified now that streaming services such as Netflix can be played through consoles to get the same visual quality graphics provided by all that processing power.

The platforms can give a different feel, reach diverse audiences and inform the desired experience even though the demographics of players will vary depending on the device they play on. Almost all industry executives agree that the most successful games will be those that work cross-platform. League of Legends by Riot Games and Fortnite by Epic Games are both cases in point.

So, what makes a game great?

It's as easy as 1-2-3.

1. Easy to pick up
2. Hard to master
3. Fun to watch

Simple in essence,
but exceptionally hard to execute.

Gaming as entertainment

It's not just the *playing* of games that is a burgeoning industry. Gaming is becoming a mainstream form of entertainment - yes, there is a growing trend for watching other people play games. Maybe it's excellent players competing against each other or in teams (esports). Maybe it's garnering top tips, or getting glimpses into future games, or just plain fun commentary. Either way, gaming is becoming a giant global social network where people spend time together and get connected.

The network is huge, as Mitch Berman, who has worked across the Hollywood studios, as well as the domestic and international launch of pay television services, knows. Mitch seems to like the shock factor when he shares the numbers with friends.

Mitch Berman explains:

"When I'm out at parties with my generation - old guys who have been there/done that in the studios and Hollywood - and I start talking about the YouTube influencers, typically what I get from these guys is: 'Oh come on Mitch, no one's going to watch that crap.'

"I take my phone out and tell one of them to read out loud to the others how many subscribers Vanoss has on YouTube. 'He's got 24 million?! What the hell?!'"

Mainstream TV doesn't broadcast gaming, yet, so where are people watching? Two platforms stand over and above any others: Twitch and YouTube. To give some perspective on the size of these platforms, twitchtracker.com clocked 949,138,028 hours of gaming watched on Twitch in January 2019 alone. But that's only half the story as YouTube accounts for around 40% of gaming video content viewers. Combined, that's a LOT of hours watched.

Globally, the number of gaming viewers reached 666 million in 2017[6] and this number is expected to have grown by at least 10% in 2019. That's a big number, especially when considering Netflix had more than 148 million streaming subscribers worldwide in the fourth quarter of 2018.

It not just time; it's money too. It is estimated that 80% of consumer spending on gaming in the US goes to content[7], which is probably why there is almost no traditional advertising - virtually all marketing is done on Twitch and through influencer networks.

Top three games streamed on both Twitch and YouTube:
- *Fortnite*
- *League of Legends*
- *PUBG* (PlayerUnknown's Battlegrounds)

[6] SuperData Research, 2017.
[7] Entertainment Software Association, 2017.

Photo credit: Casimiro PT / Shutterstock.com

Show me the money

Disguised Toast, aka Jeremy Wang, is a 27-year-old living in Beverly Hills. He is a full-time gaming influencer who streams on YouTube and Twitch. He lives with friends and fellow live streamers who are part of Offline TV, a collection of social content creators.

Curious about how much a popular gaming influencer live streamer can earn? He gives a candid insight into how he earns the money that has given him a net worth of $2million at such a young age.

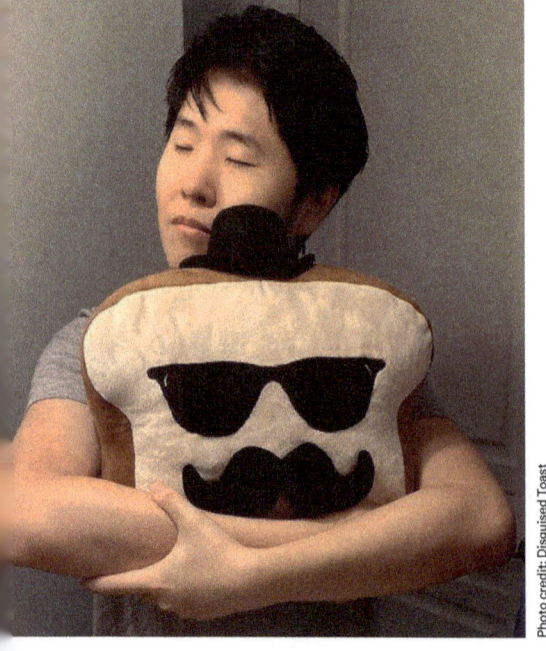

Approximate monthly salary: $20k/month plus advertising revenues and brand deals.

1. Tips/donations from viewers (direct credit card or PayPal): $2500/month.

2. Subscriptions (which cost $4.99/month of which Twitch pays out half, even those they give away for free with Amazon Prime membership): $14000/month.

Disguised Toast followers

Twitch followers: 800k (and regularly gets 10k concurrent viewers)

YouTube followers: 700k

3. Ad revenues from pre-roll ads (on Twitch he has the option to trigger ads during the stream to earn more but rarely does): $4,000/month.

4. Sponsorship revenues which can be a sponsored stream (i.e. paid to play a certain game which pays 1c to $1 per viewer), sponsored videos on YouTube (circa $5000 for a video with a 30 second ad), a live appearance at an event ($5000-$10000) all of which usually include some kind of sponsored Tweet or Instagram post. He doesn't disclose how much this equates to, but being paid the low end of a sponsored stream at 1c/viewer nets him $1000/hr.

Speaking to friends in the same industry, Jeremy confirms that the rates he has given are consistent with those that have 500 viewers and 50,000 viewers per stream. Not bad revenue streams for doing something you love in a place you love, with a community which clearly loves him. Maybe it's time for a change of career for the rest of us?

LA: the gaming incubator

Los Angeles is a city built on entertainment, and as such it supports artists and creative endeavours. It's a perfect storm of entertainment and technology, ideal for what many know as 'Silicon Beach'.

It's an ideal landing spot because of its creative nature for game design and artistry, and the industry's overall desire to collaborate. Los Angeles welcomes you wherever you are from and no matter what your idea is. After all, nobody is from LA.

The residents of this city tend to be early adopters who embrace not only new technology, but also new ways of working and consuming content. It's also a diverse population so it's easy to find what Facebook would call the 'lookalike audience' of a target demographic to test games on. As Jimmy Yun at Section Studios points out, it's not a coincidence that League of Legends, created in LA where there is a huge Korean population, became one of the most popular games in Korea.

Because a number of successful gaming companies have been built in Los Angeles, VCs interested in the space now have more presence in the city.

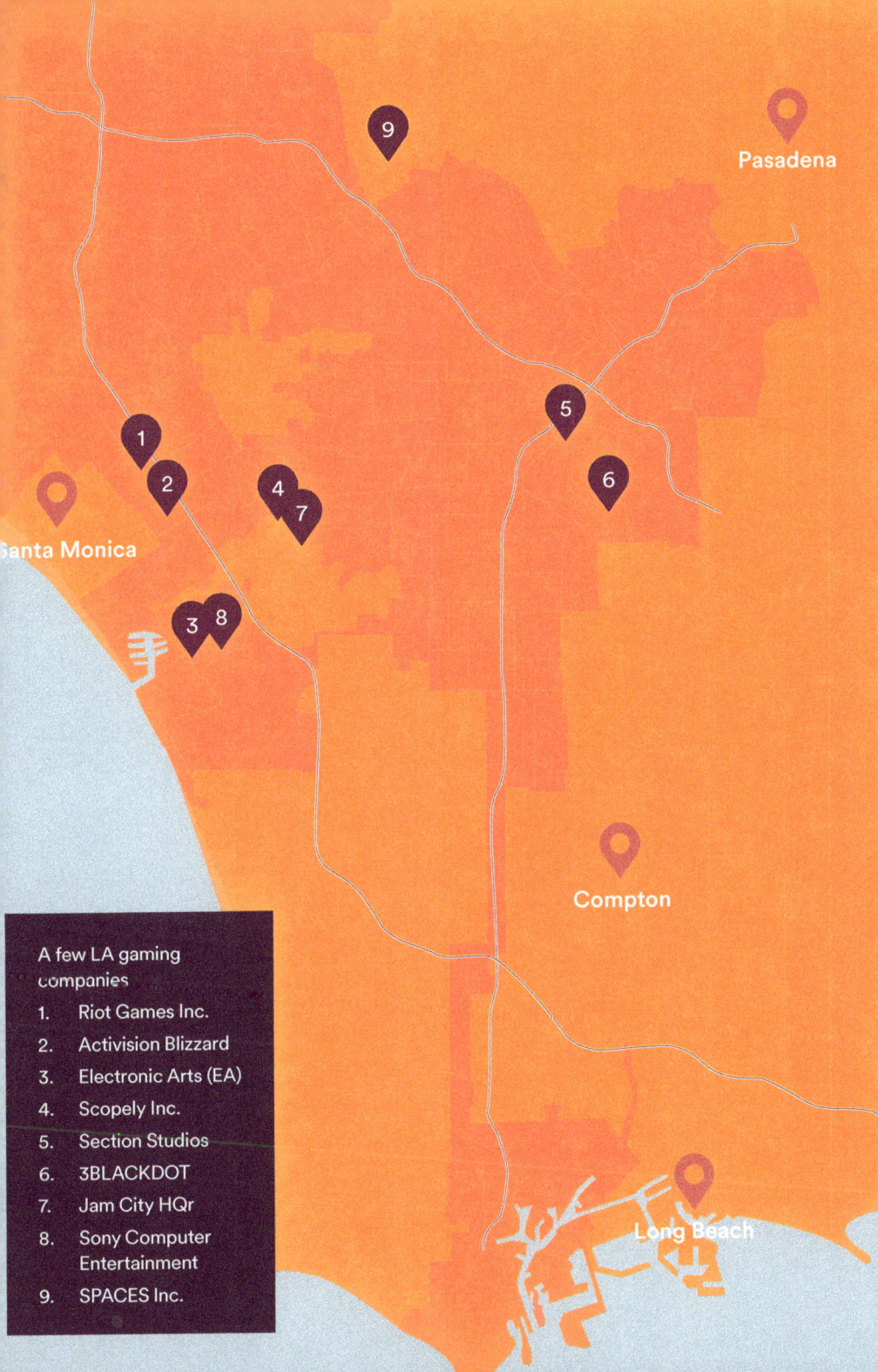

Life's a riot

Riot Games is one of the jewels in Los Angeles' crown. It was founded in 2006 by two University of Southern California (USC) college roommates who launched their first and most popular product in 2009. By 2015, it had been fully acquired by Tencent for an undisclosed sum. Riot now has 24 offices around the world and employs around 2,500 staff.

So, what makes this company unique? The founders, Brandon Beck and Marc Merrill, wanted to change the way games were developed. Rather than subscribe to the existing build/release/sell cycle, they wanted to continually optimise a single game, giving it a much longer life cycle. A successful game builds a community, and they felt developers should be part of that community, listening to feedback and releasing new features. As gamers, they also felt strongly that players shouldn't be able to buy what others achieved with skill. Therefore, all 'upgrades' are to personalise and augment a player's experience, not to advance in the game. Even when parting with money, players have said they feel as if they are gifting the money; they don't feel cheated nor taken advantage of, or that it is a necessary evil, as many view advertisements on free-to-watch platforms. Riot released League of Legends (a multiplayer battle game) in 2009.

Photo credit: Riot Games

Riot Games 'accidentally' created esports, explains Bruno Schirch, Managing Director of International Riot:

"I've been flying all over the world, and I've been able to see first-hand the passion from our community coming together and really wanting this. That was never fabricated by Riot; it all happened in the opposite way of what goes on in today's market, where many companies start with 'let's make a game for esports'. We did everything in response to what our players were asking us for - they loved it, and we saw the game really works well as a sport due to its competitive nature and how fun it is to watch.

Photo credit: Riot Games

Every single game of League of Legends is different, and there's always a distinct strategy and a social component within each game of how you are going to play as a team. As we began running tournaments, it started to be really fun, and we were not taking it too seriously. I think the first big eye openers were some of our events that we initially did in LA. We sold out an arena at USC first, and then we sold out the Staples Center, which seats 21,000 people. So, we started building professional leagues and local ecosystems around the world, but it was a long, gradual road of organic growth driven by the demand from our community."

Riot Games' The League of Legends World Championship was 2018's biggest tournament by live viewership hours on Twitch, with 53.8 million hours also producing $1.9 million in ticket sales[8].

Photo credit: Riot Games

But what about esports?

With all this popularity in gaming and access to games across platforms, esports grew organically. It was built organically from within the gaming industry in 2010 by Riot (see breakout box). The fan base for esports is expected to grow to 450 million in 2019[9] - that's over 100 million more than the entire population of the USA.

Esports tournaments draw in huge crowds, making it ripe for media and brand investments. Ben Wibberley of DAQA says:

"There are very few audiences that invoke passion more than video games and sports. By putting those two things together, you have something truly unique."

[8] newszoo, 2019. [9] Futuresource Consulting.

There is a formal structure of leagues which are highly specialised by game, and players rarely cross over. Yvette Martinez at ESL, the largest of the esports leagues, likens the esports teams to track and field: shot put is different to hurdle in the same way that League of Legends is different to Overwatch. However, she notes that these leagues are for teams only at the moment, not competitive gaming for individuals.

According to Newszoo in 2019, $897.2 million in revenues, or 82% of the total market, will come from investments such as media rights, advertising and sponsorship, and this is expected to increase to $1.5 billion by 2022, making up 87% of total esports revenues. To put this into perspective, the FIFA World Cup earned $3 billion from the World Cup culminating in 2018, which includes the years running up to the tournament.

Just like FIFA, esports are building long-term brands. These are 7-10-year plans. These teams are the new Manchester United, New York Yankees and LA Lakers.

Unlike traditional sports, esports is digitally native. The games themselves are literal new worlds built specifically to have content, character and storylines. They bring more of a social component where fans can connect easily, watch teams practice, and discuss real time in online forums, no matter where in the world they are. And Gen Z is the first truly digitally native generation. They live online and see gaming as a form of entertainment.

Team Gen.G

Photo credit: Gen G

So, how does Los Angeles play a part in this?

LA serves as a bridge between development in the US and the largest esports markets of Asia. Chris Park moved from his EVP position at Major League Baseball in New York to become CEO of Gen G esports. He says:

> "It makes sense for a lot of the teams to be here in LA because so many of the crossover opportunities require being adjacent to entertainment and to the development."

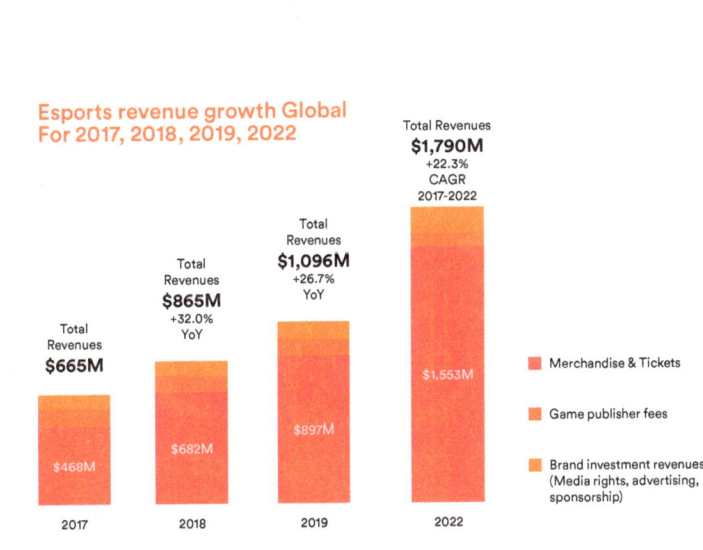

Esports revenue growth Global For 2017, 2018, 2019, 2022

Total Revenues **$665M** — 2017 — $468M

Total Revenues **$865M** +32.0% YoY — 2018 — $682M

Total Revenues **$1,096M** +26.7% YoY — 2019 — $897M

Total Revenues **$1,790M** +22.3% CAGR 2017-2022 — 2022 — $1,553M

- Merchandise & Tickets
- Game publisher fees
- Brand investment revenues (Media rights, advertising, sponsorship)

Chart source: newszoo, 2019 Global Esports Market Report

Will gaming bring virtual reality into the mainstream?

Gamers are early adopters, and the virtual reality (VR) industry had high hopes that this would be the community that made VR mainstream. I remember getting a sneak peak of Sony Morpheus for use with PlayStation before it came out, and fighting with the team for who played what next.

It was assumed that the ability to fully immerse yourself in a world would particularly appeal to gamers. However, that didn't quite happen. Maybe the cost of the hardware has been too prohibitive, needing not only a VR headset, at a cost of $130-$500 each, but also a console or PC that has high processing power and could easily set you back upwards of $3,000.

Not everyone blames the hardware, though. Perhaps gamers would have been persuaded to make this investment had a knockout game come to market? An expert in location-based VR experiences, Anthony Jacobson of Spaces, told me:

"[VR Gaming] content hasn't had that halo moment - one where it's something so special that the word of mouth creates a consumer phenomenon."

Even as hardware costs inevitably fall, will the everyday consumer have 10m²+ of open, unencumbered space needed to fully benefit from the medium? Probably not is the theory of companies such as Spaces, Dreamscape and The Void, which are all pushing high fidelity experiences in their permanent locations.

Besides, Anthony tells me that most people don't think about the technology itself as much as the experience they are about to have. This is often their first touchpoint with VR and they don't see it as gaming per se, nor do they perceive themselves as gamers. Audience demographics and times of visits are very much emblematic of the movies; earlier in the day is family-based, and, as it gets later, there are more dates and groups of friends.

Ultimately, VR may be the difference between going to a cinema and watching a film at home. But for now, location-based VR gives you something you simply cannot get at home.

Let's not forget that augmented reality (AR) has huge potential as it's mostly mobile phone enabled. AR layers on computer-generated images to the real world through a lens, such as a camera, to create an immersive experience. This lends itself to gaming - remember the Pokemon phenomenon? A few LA-based companies are looking at how more can be produced in conjunction with the real world, so watch this space for developments.

Gaming is still leading the way for VR and AR, but there are many more exciting developments to look forward to. If you're in LA, make sure you visit Dreamscape, Spaces or The Void to check out what's to come. I promise you won't be disappointed.

The big boys: who will be the Netflix of gaming?

Given the size of the industry, it won't come as a huge surprise to you that platforms, as well as traditional technology and games companies, are working to establish themselves as the online destination for gamers. They saw how Netflix irreparably damaged Hollywood and want to get ahead of the competition, especially now that 5G is imminent - giving users increased bandwidth will allow much greater fidelity and lower latency.

Here's a selection of the companies that have recently started offering a Netflix-type 'all you can eat for a set monthly fee':

Perhaps one of the best companies positioned in this area is Google (surprise, surprise). Their new **Stadia** service operates through their Chrome browser, which is already the dominant internet browser with 44% of the market[10], and promises high resolution of 4K. The Stadia service can be switched instantly between any device that has a browser, be it laptop, tablet or TV, and doesn't require additional hardware, though they will be releasing a controller.

"The worlds of watching and playing a game converge into a new generation game platform," says Phil Harrison, who heads Stadia at Google. "Our vision for Stadia is simple: one place for all the ways we play. It's focused on gamers, inspired by developers, and amplified by YouTube developers."

[10] Stetic, April 2019

Note Phil's mention of 'amplified by YouTube developers.' Google is launching "Crowd Play" on Stadia, which allows fans of video game streamers to play with their favourite online personalities while they're live on YouTube, simply by pressing 'join this game' - an incredibly smart way of allowing seamless transitions between playing and entertainment.

Apple has announced **Apple Arcade**, a video game subscription service available across all Apple devices linked to the same iCloud account, working across iPhone, iPad, Mac, and Apple TV. This is clearly aimed at mobile gamers. They are offering a service with no ads or in-app purchase for games, offline access to games, and, through a family account, up to six family members can have access. Apple's strong stance on data privacy means that personal data is not shared with developers.

Similarly, Snap announced **Snap Games**, a free-to-play, ad-supported service within the Snapchat app that focuses on shared experience with friends. Their gaming service includes messaging systems and voice chat alongside the multiplayer games, but it started fairly small, launching with just six games.

Facebook, on the other hand, has included gaming on its platform for years - remember Farmville? Many games on Facebook get more than 10 million players every day. Their **Instant Games** features more than 1,000 games that can be played with friends directly within Facebook Messenger. They are now adding a Gaming tab to the main navigation.

Sony Interactive Entertainment launched **PlayStation Now** back in 2014. It's a $19.99/month service that allows streaming access to all PlayStation Games on their devices, and those with the more recent PlayStation 4 can also download for offline playing. Non-PlayStation consoles can get access to Now with certain hardware add-ons. Game subscription services brought in $273 million during 2018's third quarter, 52% of which was attributed to PlayStation Now[11].

Microsoft, which owns Xbox, is launching **Project xCloud**, another cloud-based streaming service that allows users to play Xbox games across devices. This opens up to people who do not have dedicated gaming hardware, something which is great for developers as they can scale across devices, and could make this a serious contender for more serious gamers alongside PlayStation, Now, and Stadia.

[11] SuperData report 2018

TL;DR

- If you meet anyone who doesn't see this as a huge industry, look at them sympathetically and remind them that more than half of the US population play games on their phone, almost 1 billion hours of gaming were watched in a single month on a single platform, and the industry will shortly be worth $174 billion. Plus individual games earn significantly more revenue than Hollywood blockbusters.

- Esports is a buzzword and is set to generate billions of dollars in coming years, though this will be just a fraction of overall gaming revenues.

- Gaming uses the influencer networks like no other industry. Great gaming influencers, such as Vanoss, have 24 million subscribers on YouTube. Even with a smaller audience, Disguised Toast earns more than $20k/month.

- Los Angeles has everything in place for gaming: talent, Hollywood storytelling and brands, a diverse audience, direct access to influencers, plus proximity to Silicon Valley tech and to large audiences in Asia.

- The same disruption that came to music and TV is coming to gaming - all-access for a fixed monthly fee, aka the Netflix model. With the benefit of seeing other industries move through this disruption, more gaming companies are ready and launching competitive services around the same time, just as internet speeds improve dramatically with the launch of 5G.

Retail

The changing shape of retail

I didn't coin the term 'retailtainment', though I wish I had. We all like to be entertained, even when we're shopping. *Especially* **when we are shopping. Purchases are often emotional - which brands do you connect with the most? Which make you feel good? And when was the last time you bought something from someone you didn't like? Even if that happened recently, I suspect you won't be going back in a hurry.**

So, if we want to be entertained and buy - quite literally - into the story of a brand, product or service, where better to do that than in the home of Hollywood?

One of the best-known examples of storytelling marketing in Los Angeles is Dollar Shave Club. Founded in 2011, it all started with a quirky video featuring the founder introducing the service for $1/month and telling viewers that 'the razors aren't good, they're f***ing great'. Google the video now - it's just 90 seconds of your time, and it's really quite funny.

It's a simple story, cheaply made and well-executed. This video has had more than 26 million views. By 2016, Dollar Shave Club had 1 million customers buying low-priced razors on a subscription basis, and sold to Unilever for $1 billion. Not a bad return on the $163.5 million they had raised in total. Unilever had a lot to learn from Dollar Shave Club about online customer acquisition and creating a brand that resonated with its audience.

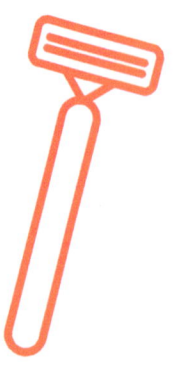

Retail

In recent years, this model of direct-to-consumer (D2C) has become commonplace, bypassing retail outlets completely. From Bonobos' clothes, Casper's mattresses and The Honest Company's cleaning and baby products, to new categories, such as complete-meal-in-a-bottle provider Soylent, D2C brands have now hit every major market. So, if everyone is buying online, does that mean offline retail is dead?

Far from it. We're actually coming full circle. With so many brands out there, consumers often want to touch or feel a product before they buy. In fact, this is becoming so important that many D2C brands are now setting up in bricks and mortar. Perhaps one of the first to do this successfully was Warby Parker, which set up as a D2C brand, but, after finding success with a flagship store, now makes more money from bricks-and-mortar retailing than they make online.

More and more brands are moving towards an omnichannel approach (in-store, online, by phone and through social media) to maximise their sales potential.

With this new confluence of media, marketing and manufacturing changing the landscape for retail, it's worth a look at some of the stand-out companies and trends that are changing the way we shop.

Photo credit: YouTube, Dollar Shave Club

The celebrity entrepreneurs

A fast-growing trend in Los Angeles is celebrities founding their own businesses. Brian Furano knows this space inside out. He runs Business Development at LA-based memBrain, which connects celebrities and large brands for media, marketing and retail purposes, developing and executing entertainment, marketing and media programmes for major brands.

Brian has witnessed first-hand how the role of celebrity involvement with big brands and companies is changing. He continues: "We regularly see celebrities appear in adverts and marketing campaigns for large brands, and a celebrity tweet or sponsored post can spark sudden growth for a product. But, in the last few years, savvy celebrities have gone much further.

At some point over the past decade, A-list stars and emerging personalities began to realise their power to build communities and engagement around a product or company. But, instead of simply endorsing a product for a fee, celebrities began building brands from the ground up.

For many celebrities, particularly in the landscape of 2019, the brands they align with or build must reflect their values and what they want to represent.

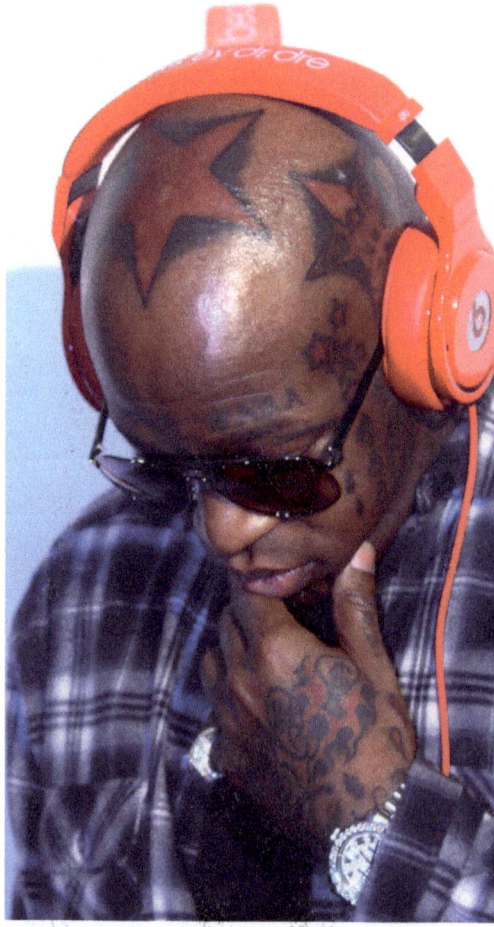

Rapper Birdman wearing Beats By Dr Dre & Lil Wayne

Photo credit: RoidRanger / Shutterstock.com

"Before Ashton Kutcher and Twitter, 50 Cent and Vitamin Water, Snoop and Reddit, and Beats by Dre, the world of celebrity endorsements was limited to advertising brand spokesperson engagements" Brian says. *"Never have we seen such a large number of celebrities, athletes, influencers, and thought leaders becoming meaningful partners with big business and founder/owners themselves."*

Black Panther star Michael B. Jordan has collaborated with Brisk Iced Tea in launching an arts programme. Jaden Smith, along with his father Will Smith, launched an eco-friendly, pollution-reducing water company, Just Water. And actress Kate Hudson's sportswear and healthy lifestyle brand, Fabletics, has made an enormous splash on the world stage."

See also: Gwyneth Paltrow's lifestyle brand, Goop; Reese Witherspoon's media company, Hello Sunshine; Will.i.Am's fashion-tech company, i.am+, and Jessica Alba's non-toxic home goods line, The Honest Company - all built in LA.

So, what makes these brands more successful than standard advertising endorsements? I asked Brian. "Their hearts are all in. There is no online backlash around authenticity. These celebrities are building their enterprises from a truthful and meaningful place."

There is another way in which celebrities are becoming involved in enterprise. Several of them invest in companies in a more behind-the-scenes way. Ashton Kutcher is a well-known investor in LA, as are Jay Z and Magic Johnson, to name a few.

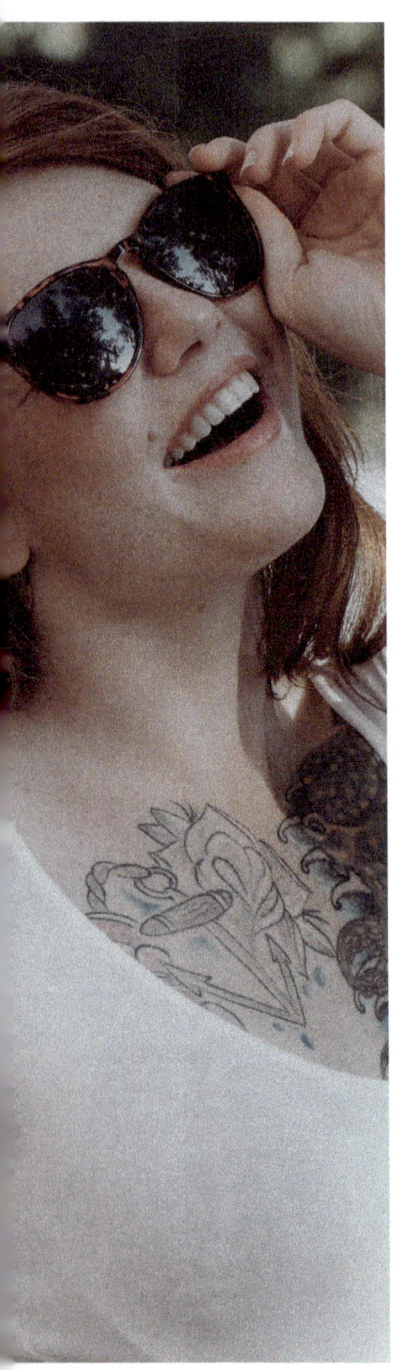

Why conscience matters

People want to feel good about what they are buying - and what better way to feel good about something than if you are helping someone else in the process? Some 87% of consumers say that they will buy a product because the company which made it is involved with an issue they care about[1].

TOMS shoes were the first to tap into this sentiment. The company was founded by Blake Mycoskie in 2006 after he visited Argentina and witnessed the hardships there, in particular seeing children walking miles without shoes. He launched his company with a simple premise: for every pair of shoes purchased, TOMS would provide new shoes for a child in need. No strings attached. They sold 10,000 pairs of shoes in their first year; the shoes they gave away were distributed through a humanitarian organisation as part of a wider community development programme.

You can see the first iterations of the shoes at the company head office in Silicon Beach, a cool, high-ceiled warehouse space complete with a mock shop display showing off their current range, swing chairs, and a slide between floors. In a mini amphitheatre, they show groups the evolution of their shoes, and how different versions are donated for different terrains and seasons.

[1] 2017 Cone Communications CSR Study

Just a few miles away, on fashionable Abbot Kinney Boulevard, is TOMS' flagship store. Here, TOMS sells shoes, eyewear and bags, and there's an in-store coffee shop where hipsters hang out with their MacBooks.

All retail purchases have a 'giving' angle. Sales of eyewear help provide prescription glasses, medical treatment, and/or sight-saving surgery to people in need. Sales of coffee provide 140 litres of safe water (a one-week supply) to a person in need. Sales of bags help provide training for birth attendants and the distribution of birth kits containing items that help a woman to safely deliver her baby (as of 2016, TOMS say they have supported safe birth services for more than 25,000 mothers globally).

This mission-led approach has revolutionised corporate social responsibility in the retail space, evolving into a powerful business model which has been replicated the world over by brands such as Warby Parker, Figs, Bixby, and many others.

LA: the manufacturing city

One of the reasons D2C is thriving in Los Angeles is that it's the biggest manufacturing hub in the country. Roughly one third of all US-based manufacturers are in LA County. Yes, I was surprised too.

This springs partly from WWII, when Los Angeles became a production hub for war supplies. Aside from the amount of space, there are exceptional transportation links with the ports of LA and Long Beach, and LAX airport, offering shipping via road and rail to the rest of California and the wider US for inbound and outbound components and products.

Los Angeles, being home to a plethora of industries, means the manufacturing that serves them embraces many different specialties, from fabricated metal to transportation equipment and apparel. This has worked in the city's favour, since it can be difficult to move plants elsewhere when there is reliance on other specialist skills/components for the end product.

Transporting different components between factories can be cumbersome and expensive, not to mention extremely detrimental to the environment. Also, if there is a problem with one part of the manufacturing cycle, it's a lot easier to hop in a car and visit a plant than it is to deal with it on the phone, or have to travel to another part of the country.

'Sustainability' and 'local' are two words you hear a lot in LA - business owners often talk about paths to sustainability and 'going green'. Maybe they are mission-led, maybe they appreciate that it's good marketing/PR - either way, the trend to more sustainable products and services has been steadily growing.

This may be why the HQ of the Clean Energy Smart Manufacturing Innovation Institute (CESMII) is in LA, helping all companies to produce more efficiently.

Jim Davis, Vice Provost IT, Chief Academic Technology Officer and Principal Investigator and CIO Advisor at CESMII, explains:

"Smart manufacturing is using data to create better products, improve how products are managed, and reduce the energy and materials used. It is doing so more safely and with less impact on the environment."

In other words, manufacturing processes are improving across just about every metric, all the time.

Los Angeles is home to a vast number of brands which manufacture locally and are vocal about it - particularly when it comes to fashion. More than 80% of US jeans are made in Los Angeles, for example.

Mixing it up: retail, entertainment and commerce

FabFitFun has almost come full circle. It started in 2010 as an online magazine lifestyle brand and community for beauty, fashion, fitness, and wellness - all very LA. Just a few years after launch, they noticed the popularity of subscription boxes. Consumers were delighted at the perceived discounted value they would get on a set of curated products - usually trail size - to be sent direct to their door each month.

The companies behind the subscription boxes either agreed highly-discounted rates with brands as part of their marketing spend, or, for the most successful, sold the privilege of placing a product in their box to a highly-qualified audience, thus helping products 'get discovered'.

FabFitFun had a highly desired audience in place and strong connections with brands through their advertising teams. They were going to LA-based events and receiving VIP gift bags with full-size products. They saw an opportunity to replicate the subscription boxes and, in 2013, trialed a quarterly 'seasonal' box modelled on VIP 'gift bags'. They planned for 2,000 bags and had sold out within two days.

The FabFitFun boxes have full-size products and allow consumers to customise their boxes through certain choices of product. This not only allows individuals to get the most relevant products, considered a steal at $49.99 for a value of around $200, but also gives FabFitFun data points of preference for different demographics.

They don't just sell this as a subscription box. FabFitFun is a membership. People are buying into a community.

In addition to the boxes, members receive a wealth of content. FabFitFun has its own in-house studios with shows including health, wellness, fitness, cooking and relationships. It has its own work-outs, cooking shows, and more. Live shows appear on platforms, such as Facebook, and there's an app for AppleTV and Amazon Fire.

FabFitFun has now branched out from beauty and fitness to home, fashion, health and wellness. Growth rates have been as high as 300% year-on-year.

FabFitFun also works as a commerce platform, allowing people to buy more of their favourite products: members get priority and early access to desirable brands. The company has taken a leaf out of Amazon's book, creating own-brand products based on all the data points they already have, which, in turn, gives much higher margins. Brands include ISH, Summer & Rose and Chic & Tonic. Is it a retail business? A marketing business? An entertainment business? In truth, it's all three.

Photo credit: FabFitFun

Personalisation and paying online rent

eSalon is one of my favourite LA-based companies. It's highly successful and has taken no outside investment. I use their products, and there are a number of reasons I think this company is particularly innovative. Mainly, though, I find their story unusual.

eSalon is a personalised hair dye company, whose CEO is bald. The business came about after a discussion between friends over dinner. How does it cost $200+ to get hair dyed in a salon when packaged dye costs $10 in the local shop? The difference, it seemed, was that the salon personalised the hair colour, mixing it there and then to give the desired look.

Could it be that difficult to personalise hair dye on a mass scale? As some of the most detail-oriented people I have come across, they set about researching ingredients and building a prototype assembly. They tinkered, day in, day out, until they got it right. Their customers subscribe to receive a regular supply of hair dye personalised to them. The box arrives with personalised instructions and everything that's needed to get the hair colour they have chosen - from the dye to gloves, stain guard, and specialised shampoo and conditioner.

We hear a lot about the personalisation of consumer products, but mostly this involves a customer choosing a specific pattern, shape, size, or frequency. True personalisation involves many different variables. If you consider all the different elements of this product - the thousands of different colour combinations, personalised instructions, and delivery information - the margin of error is huge. Yet, the company has made no major mistakes, ensuring that every one of its 270,000 customers receives their correct formula.

eSalon has built a loyal following and made some smart moves:

- They have used social media for maximum customer acquisition, getting under the skin of their target client and their online habits. They know exactly how much it costs to acquire a new customer through targeted posts and adverts.

- Consumers sign up to eSalon online by responding to simple questions and are given the opportunity to upload photos. The company employs qualified colourists who review each new order and will send feedback and options if they think the colours the consumer has chosen will not meet their objectives.

- Consumers can decide how frequently they want to receive colour, and it's easy to skip an order, so they're not locked into a structure that doesn't suit their needs.

- They have an excellent upsell range of complementary products from hair dye tools to everyday hair care. Around 20% of their overall revenue is from non-hair colour-related products and accessories.

Photo credit: eSalon

Photo credit: eSalon

eSalon built a steady business but realised their customer acquisition costs were mounting. Their recent changes are the most innovative and the most old-school.

Tamir Buchler, another of their male executives who is challenged in the hair department but knows a lot about retail, explains: "We're paying rent online. That's really what is happening right now. Transfer this idea of a brick-and-mortar rent to acquiring users online and effectively paying rent online in our own way. So, whatever you spend to acquire customers online has now worked its way around to: 'I can afford the same amount as having a customer experience in a physical store.' [And, for this product] the physical environment lends itself to what we are trying to achieve."

After detailed analysis, eSalon opened its first fully-fledged salon.

Tamir explains: "We have owned and operated salons and studios that we're opening up. We're not looking to become the [blow] Dry Bar of hair colour; we're looking to leverage our studios as a way to acquire customers, and educate them and teach them how to use our products at home.

So, yes, it's affordable. You can walk into one of those studios and get hair colour the first time for $35, which seems ridiculously cheap, but you'll walk away with knowledge and understanding of our custom formulations, how to personalise them for you, and how to do it at home. Our goal is to get you on an auto renew programme when you walk out the door. It's happening about 90 per cent of the time."

Bridging the online and offline worlds

As more retailers become 'omnichannel', it gets harder for businesses to understand the fragmentation of audiences across channels. Physical to digital seems to be particularly challenging: who is coming to the store? What are they looking at? What do they go on to buy online? Retailers need answers to these questions, but they are not technology companies - and building out solutions is not their wheelhouse.

As Amanda Latifi, Founder of Hafta Have, which helps retailers drive traffic and conversion through existing methods, puts it:

"Essentially, [retailers] have no idea what's going on in the store until the consumer makes a purchase."

With seemingly boundless energy and a vast knowledge of integrated marketing across digital platforms, Amanda saw an opportunity: "When I started Hafta Have, the co-founder of the company, whom I consider to be a mentor, told me that, if I was taking this seriously, I needed to relocate to [San Francisco] Bay from Los Angeles."

Amanda ignored his advice because she loves living in Los Angeles. She is delighted that she did, since she rarely needs to be in San Francisco; all of her business is in LA and New York.

Hafta Have started as an app and was immediately successful. If, like me, you don't always want to try things on when you're shopping, or don't want to carry bags of purchases around all afternoon, you take a picture of the label for future reference. Hafta Have's app allowed you to do just that, but more effectively. Working with 120 retailers, including Gap and Lululemon, consumers could automatically register the photo with the appropriate retailer, which could then match size and local availability to your profile and give access to any of the retailers' current offers.

Then retailers started coming to Hafta Have for their data. Who were these users? When were they shopping? Where? Amanda quickly realised that Hafta Have was the only company out there where data from in-store indicated an intent to buy online.

To make it easier for consumers, they scrapped the need to download the Hafta Have app and switched to simple text messaging. Amanda explains: "Shoppers in-store can take a picture of a price tag. They text it to a short code. We add that item to a digital list of things they have purchase intent against. We link the product data on the digital side, then the retailer can start using their existing online targeting to convert to a sale."

Once a retailer has a customer's phone number and knows what they want to buy, it can tie this information into traditional targeting through online and social platforms.

Amanda has become an expert in retail data. She told me about a large retailer looking to downsize by closing some shops. To decide which ones should close, they looked at the least profitable stores, which sounds like it makes perfect sense. However, they had only looked at in-store sales, and hadn't taken into account the online sales generated by each store. When they factored all sales into the equation, their choice of which store to close changed entirely.

Instant gratification: I need it NOW

I'm getting spoilt as a shopper. Once I know what I want, I want it NOW! This is mostly Amazon's fault. It has set a new bar for speedy delivery, and I get grumpy if I have to wait more than a couple of days for something I've bought. Also, because I live in Los Angeles, a major hub, deliveries sometimes arrive even more quickly.

But Amazon is not the only retailer which can achieve that. Any retailer in a metropolitan area can now offer one-hour delivery by leveraging their retail stores and warehouse infrastructure alongside the new and growing networks of delivery services, such as Postmates and Doordash. And that's thanks to LA-based Shipsi, which has combined them into one "mega-network" that brands and retailers can directly integrate into their native systems.

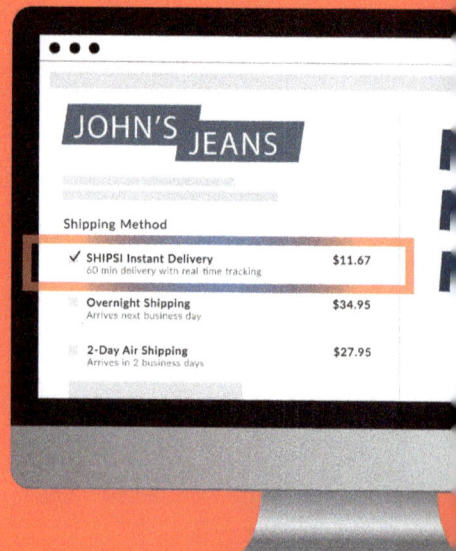

Photo credit: Shipsi

It works as follows on a Shipsi customer website:

- When a consumer gets to check out, the integrated systems check for local inventory.

- If inventory is available, an additional delivery option offering one- or two-hour delivery will be given.

- Shipsi aggregates last-mile delivery networks, such as Uber and Postmates, which effectively 'bid', giving a real-time cost to pick up the order and deliver it within the designated time. The cheapest bid is shown to the consumer.

- If the consumer chooses the one- or two- hour delivery window, the merchandise is picked up in-store or from a nearby warehouse/ distribution centre by the delivery company and delivered to the customer.

Photo credit: Shipsi

Chelsie Lee is another dynamic leader who is passionate about what she does. Sitting in her all-white office drinking sparkling water, she's animated about the benefits this brings to the consumer and retailer alike.

She explains that, by using the Shipsi service, retailers save, not only on standard shipping, but also on the packaging of the item in preparation for shipment. Therefore, some of them pass on all or part of these savings to the consumer. In most cases, it's actually cheaper to use Shipsi than to use regular delivery, so the retailer benefits from lower postage costs and the consumer benefits by receiving their merchandise quickly.

By using the Shipsi service, brands can also have a presence in areas where they don't have retail outlets. Shipsi works with warehouses and fulfilment centres in more than 600 cities and 1 million drivers across the US.

For brands and retailers, it's not just the service and the access to new areas that's crucial: it's also the data. Retailers can observe real-time responses to marketing campaigns, as their dashboard shows them what is selling, where and when. This improves agility and can be utilised to improve their entire supply chain in today's 'now commerce' era.

Returns: the pain point for online sales

One of the downsides of online shopping is that you can't touch and feel the products, or try on clothing to make sure it fits - this is particularly pertinent when a Brit like me forgets that US and UK sizes are different. Recently, I assumed (wrongly, as it turned out) I could send something back that I didn't like. I won't be purchasing from that shop again.

This isn't unique to me. The move to online shopping through visually native mediums, such as Instagram, has made it easy to shop. Perhaps too easy. And it's created a problem for retailers: customers are returning a lot of goods. Buying online means that the consumer takes a risk, especially on clothing: what if the sizing isn't what I'm expecting? What if the colour isn't what I'm expecting? Or what if I just don't like it when I see it? It's no wonder that sales through digital channels have three to four times higher return rates than sales through physical locations.

Consumer expectations are changing, partly thanks to Amazon, and people now expect free returns. In fact, 89% of shoppers check return policies before purchasing items, and 55% have chosen not to purchase an item because the return policy wasn't flexible enough. Apparently, it's not just me that's spoilt.

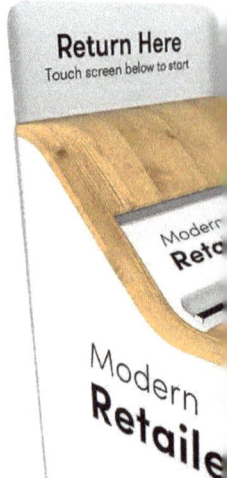

Photo credit: Happy Returns Co

For retailers, the cost of return by mail is expensive, particularly when dealing with smaller packages with very little or no information about size or weight. It's also a hassle for consumers to repack goods, find suitable packaging, print a label, and take it to an appropriate drop-off point. It's tiring just thinking about that.

Even if a retailer has a local physical presence, it may not sell the same inventory as the online store. That means returns are processed locally, but have to have a special place in-store where they sit among other one-off returns.

It's a conundrum for retailers because they don't want to encourage returns - it's much better if consumers keep everything they buy, but that's not a realistic goal, so retailers need to get their returns policy right.

Happy Returns is trying to solve this problem and has attracted well-respected US brands, such as Rothys and Everlane. The premise is simple but effective. Happy Returns has physical Return Bars in metropolitan areas across the US. Customers can return their goods in person without the need to print a label or pack up the items - they simply bring the returns and their receipt. By scanning the receipt and the items, the company gathers all the data associated with that purchase and can trigger a refund from the retailer immediately.

These returns are then aggregated and sent to one of the Happy Returns' hubs for secondary processing: getting the goods back to being sale-ready (refolding items, or removing lint or a scuff, for example). From here, the items are shipped back to the retailers' warehouse ready for resale.

As more returns are processed, Happy Returns gathers more data, which helps retailers. It's easier to spot consumers who are serial returners, and they also have a better grasp of return rates and overall data. They can benchmark against similar companies, identify spikes with specific products or specific product lines, and, because they are not waiting for postal delivery like retailers, their data is more up-to-date.

With the benefit of economies of scale, Happy Returns not only makes vast improvements to the returns process for consumers, but can also save retailers money when they're processing returns. It's no wonder they have a net promoter score of 95%.

Photo credit: Westfield

Does the mall have a future?

"Malls are dying" is something I often hear. And yes, some are closing and being put to other uses. Google, for example, will be renting a 584,000 sq ft space that was once the Westside Pavilion Mall and converting it to office space. But Los Angeles is also seeing a revitalisation of malls, with several new spaces being created or upgraded in the last few years.

Caruso is the most famous company, creating 'beloved destinations that reflect the unique fabric of the communities in which they live'. The company owns, designs and operates spaces all over Los Angeles and beyond. The best-known and most emblematic is The Grove, between Beverly Hills and West Hollywood. It has a distinctly outdoor feel along a street with a dancing fountain, outdoor cafe seating, and an old-school art deco cinema. The Wall Street Journal has rated The Grove as having the best concierge in the country. It is also one of the highest-grossing malls in the US.

Caruso's newest development, Palisades Village, is a high-end, outdoor, beautifully designed mall that opened to immediate acclaim. Food & Wine describe it as "LA's star-studded instant sensation."

One of the reasons for Caruso's success is that the company creates beautiful walking spaces in a city that is otherwise unwalkable. International chain Westfield is also capitalising on this and has started adding more services to its malls, so people can accomplish several things in one space. For example, their Century City location features several health and wellness outlets, such as Next Health (featured in the Health chapter).

In fact, Westfield is going one step further than retail and entertainment. Several of its new malls also feature living spaces and offices. US CFO Philip Slavin tells me:

"That's one of the reasons for the move towards multiple uses, not just entertainment. [To also include] the notion of residential, and working [in our malls]. I think it will move towards becoming a town centre in time - it's an evolution."

Photo credit: Westfield

Photo credit: Westfield

Successful mall owners also recognise that, in order to attract consumers, they need to have innovative new outlets within their space, in addition to well-known favourites. Several of them have therefore had to change their business model from straight monthly rent to a percentage of revenue.

As malls develop to become more forward-thinking and innovative, they're also much more aware of the technology available to improve customer experience. For example, I have signed up so that, when I drive into my local Westfield mall, my car is recognised and I am automatically billed for parking rather than having to take a ticket and go to a pay station. It's a smoother operation for me, and Westfield now has data on when I go and how long I stay. In time, this could also be combined with data from loyalty programmes to build a more complete picture of how a person shops and thus help improve engagement.

In theory, malls could go one step further and use mobile phone data or facial recognition to track my movements in the mall. This would, in turn, enable the mall owner or individual retailers to target me with enticing offers to enter the store or spend more time in a particular outlet. Facial recognition could also track my expressions - sad, happy, impatient - to indicate specific intent.

Although this technology is available, there are a number of ethical issues. Mall owners have two sets of customers, consumers and retailers, so they need to balance the needs of both. This means balancing the demands of retailers wanting customer data with consumers in a public space who do not want their every movement tracked. California is bringing in data protection laws similar to those launched in Europe recently, so many malls are waiting to decide what technologies are used, and how, even if the potential is already there.

LA malls

1. **The Grove,** a Caruso-designed mall, is one of the highest-grossing in the country. It has an outdoor feel along a street with a dancing fountain and outdoorcafe seating.
2. **The Original Farmers Market** was established in 1934 and is open seven days a week. It has 100 food stalls.
3. **Platform,** which opened in 2016, is a repurposed industrial complex that houses restaurants, offices, and work-out spaces. Tenants are asked to provide 'unique experiences' for customers, taking advantage of the new expo line running between downtown and Santa Monica and the subsidies that go with it.
4. **Westfield Century City** recently had a $1 billion makeover, bringing together retail and entertainment, including Dreamscape, one of the most forward-thinking virtual reality experiences available.
5. **The Beverly Center** was renovated in 2016 with skylights, a perforated steel exterior, and a revamped restaurant area.
6. **Santa Monica Place** reopened in 2010 after a huge refurbishment. Situated a couple of blocks from the beach with high-end stores, much of it is focused around an outdoor walkable space. It features outdoor eating areas on the roof deck and the brand new Cayton Children's Museum.
7. **Palisades Village,** which opened in 2018, is a high-end, outdoor, beautifully designed space by Caruso. Food & Wine describe it as "LA's star-studded instant sensation."
8. **Hollywood Park** is due to open in 2020 as part of a new sports stadium in Inglewood that will be home to two NFL teams: the Los Angeles Rams and the Los Angeles Chargers. It describes itself as "a sophisticated, world-class 500,000 sq ft regional community hub and lifestyle center with a future 340,000 sq ft expansion featuring retail, dining, entertainment, events, and a dynamic social culture and community."

Do we need to own anything?

As I was researching this book and came across Joymode, I joined to check it out. It's a membership service giving its customers access to all those things you may only use once or twice a year, but which take up so much room, cluttering the back of your wardrobe or collecting dust in your garage. Now I no longer own these things; I borrow them from Joymode instead, as and when I need them.

Just recently, I've borrowed camping equipment, a sous-vide machine, giant games (to entertain children at a party), a pressure washer, a VR headset, and some guest essentials for a toddler who came to stay. Joymode owns all these items: when I request them, they are delivered to and collected from my house during dedicated time slots. I love it.

So, I was delighted to meet company founder Joe Fernandez, who is truly passionate about his business. The ultimate aim of Joymode? "If we can feel like a lifestyle magazine, where you push a button and life is delivered to you, that's what we strive for. We're kind of 'the anti-retail' because you don't need to deal with a lot of stuff" Joe explains.

I wondered if my use of the company was typical. "The third most popular thing on Joymode is a vacuum cleaner, but the most popular is a backyard movie night - a screen projector and a tiny popcorn machine."

Photo credit: Joymode

Diverse communities want different things - one of the advantages of being in LA is being able to test diverse markets. Some differences are obvious: people who live by the beach don't order beach stuff because they already own it, but it's popular with people living in Hollywood or Downtown who are heading out for the day or weekend. One of the most significant indicators is whether households have children or not.

"The two neighborhoods where Joymode has most traction is downtown LA, which makes sense [because] there are a lot of early adopters there, and Beverly Wood, which is single family [homes], with a lot of people of the Orthodox Jewish faith. We serve Torrence and Koreatown, Pasadena and Malibu. They are totally different worlds, so, for us, that gives us a lot of confidence. If you can make it here [in LA], you can make it anywhere because it's not just a single set of people."

Retailers see consumer habits changing and that creates mutual opportunities with rental services.

Joymode are looking to extend the opportunities to work with other businesses. They recently partnered with Lowes, also an investor, to co-create experiences to bring members the tools they need to get household jobs done. They've also teamed up with a well-known LA restaurant to provide the equipment and food needed to create a romantic dinner at home.

Joymode's emphasis is very much on using the platform to enhance offline experiences. Joe explains that "[Joymode is] more like a logistics company and it's fun to help people connect to the real world around these products. We are creating moments where you can just go have a picnic, and we deliver the stuff to you. You know you have to connect with people in other ways. And we see people adopting that lifestyle."

Photo credit: Joymode

TL;DR

- Retail and entertainment are merging, and storytelling is key. Consumers want to know more about the brands they buy. Brands are more cognisant of owning their story across all channels, often creating their own content.

- Social media has fundamentally changed the way products and services are marketed. The cost of online customer acquisition has soared, and companies now see this as 'paying rent online'.

- Celebrities and influencers can help exponentially to grow consumer brands.

- Amazon is setting the standard for customer service. It has driven free deliveries and shortened delivery times, as well as opened the door to free returns. Successful retailers are those that compete with Amazon on a fundamental service level.

- Retailers that crack omnichannel sales, understanding their customers across online and offline platforms, will be the most successful.

- Consumers still want to experience products and services before they buy, or have an easy return policy.

- Los Angeles is such a high-consumption market with a diverse population that it's an excellent test bed for consumer products. It's one of the largest retail and fashion markets in the US.

- The fact that people spend so much time in their cars here has stimulated an appetite for experiences where they can walk, shop, be entertained and interact with others. That's why Westfield sees people spending more than six hours in their malls.

- Part of the story is about sustainability - doing something positive for the environment makes us feel good about what we are buying.

An inspiring story of innovation: how LA's gangs rocked retail

There are so many gangs in Los Angeles that they have their own list on Wikipedia. Not that most Angelenos will ever meet them, but I intended to be the exception.

I approached HomeBoy Industries and knew I was in the right place - I was a lone white face, wearing designer sunglasses and high heels, and standing out like a sore thumb among a large group of mostly Hispanic men covered in tattoos at their bakery and office in DTLA. Yes, you read that right: bakery.

Asking at the front desk for the contact I'd been given, she came down a few minutes later to greet me with a huge smile and the words 'Fuck Off' tattooed across her face. In the bubble that I live in, this would come as a shock to most people, but, given the warmth that came with it, it all made sense.

In the same bubble I live in, many people have heard about Homeboy, or they've seen the logo on clothing and merchandise at the LA City Hall Diner, at LAX Terminal 4, or at a local LA farmers' market. This brand represents the largest and most successful gang intervention, rehabilitation and re-entry programme in the world. It may also be the most humble.

One of the many pages on the LAPD website devoted to gangs states: "There are more than 450 active gangs in the City of Los Angeles. Many of these gangs have been in existence for over 50 years.

Photo credit: HomeBoy Industries

These gangs have a combined membership of over 45,000 individuals." Other reports put the total number of gang members in LA nearer to 120,000.

Gang members are often second and third generation in their family; they stay local to their neighborhood and don't get involved with outsiders, which is why most Angelenos never cross paths with them in their daily lives. To give some context to this, most gangs are on the eastern side of the city and have never travelled the 12 miles to the beach on the west side. Similarly, I live on the west side and only get to the east side every few weeks.

In 1988, Father Greg Boyle decided to take a new approach to helping gang members and ex-felons forge a different lifestyle, by treating them as individuals "capable of healing and transformation."

The violent reputation of gangs made it difficult to fundraise on their behalf and for Father Boyle to find suitable jobs for the people he helped. He fundamentally believed that facilitating this group of people to get the training they needed, and the resulting work opportunities, offered a way out of the gang culture. This path had never existed before. Father Boyle created HomeBoy Industries to do exactly that.

At HomeBoy Industries HQ, Omar has volunteered to take me on a tour to give me the background and his personal story. I glance at his arm in a sling and make a cursory comment about his injury.

"Oh, it's so much better than it was. It's from the brain damage when I was shot."

When Omar saw my horror and sadness at what he'd been through, he simply smiled and told me that many people here had been shot at one time or another.

Omar tells his story of growing up in a gang culture. He assumed he'd be dead by the age of 18 and didn't value his life as a result: no one else seemed to, so why should he? He was first introduced to Homeboy when he was 12 and visited several times over the following years. After he'd been shot, which at first confined him to a wheelchair and created several long-term health issues, including challenges with his speech and permanent damage to his right arm, Omar was ready to commit full-time to the programme at Homeboy. He was 19 and still alive, so he'd gotten further and lived longer than he ever thought he would.

Omar's story isn't unique.

Some 90% of people who come through the programme at Homeboy have never held down a 'real' job, giving them no basis for a work ethic. Some 30 to 40% are homeless, either couch surfing, looking for hostels or temporary accommodation, or sleeping on the street.

HomeBoy Industries supported almost 8,000 people in 2018 and is now a $20 million organisation. The majority of revenue comes from donations. In Los Angeles, there are a number of successful entrepreneurs who have had mentors to help them along the way, and that mentorship resonates with the work being done by Homeboy.

Father Greg Boyle not only provides this much-needed mentorship, but he and the staff have also managed to create a space where individuals feel so safe that rival gang members work side by side - a remarkable achievement.

Photo credit: HomeBoy Industries

My time with Omar immediately reflected this. During a Criminals and Gang Members Anonymous session, he listened to a rival gang member open up about his life, talking about his challenges and showing vulnerability. Omar quickly recognised himself and learned that he shared many of the same issues. The experience helped him to start to see this person as a fellow human rather than the enemy he had always thought him to be. As Father Greg says: "Hard to demonise someone you know."

The programme, which hosts around 400 people a year, lasts 18 months and is paid, so participants are supported while they learn and try to reset their lives. The first part of the programme is focused on personal development. As one graduate of the programme puts it: "I like to say we come here to unlearn, to relearn in a new way."

The second part of the programme focuses on the participants getting workforce training and building job skills within the social enterprise businesses that are part of the organisation. These job development skills can be transferred, hence the title 'Industries'.

The social enterprise businesses give Homeboy a large portion of revenue - around $7 million per year, which CEO Thomas Vozzo explains could be double. However, Homeboy employs twice the number of staff members as would a for-profit business. The main purpose of the organisation, even within the social enterprises, is healing and job training.

Through the programme, participants receive free wraparound services that include tattoo removal, legal and mental health support, educational services, workforce development support and case management. Classes at Homeboy range from Alcoholics Anonymous, to preparing for life with Project Fatherhood and Work Readiness to the highly practical Building Your First Budget and Employment Assistance. One of the most noteworthy of the services offered by Homeboy is tattoo removal. The organisation provided 11,240 tattoo removal sessions in 2018, to be exact.

Beyond the individual services it offers, Homeboy provides a safe space for individuals to come without fear of judgement; somewhere they are treated as equals and supported in understanding the trauma and pain that they carry. It is a place where people can examine their lives and their self-worth, so they can start to understand their resilience, find their strengths, and move forward to healing. The place provides an environment filled with lessons from which all of us could benefit.

Health
& Wellness

Looking good, feeling great

Where I come from in the UK, there is a pub on every corner. In Los Angeles, there is a yoga studio on every corner. Angelenos are much more aware of their health, both physically and mentally.

LA has rubbed off on me. I no longer have a fridge full of cheese and champagne; it's now stocked with kale and sparkling water. Every morning, I make a green smoothie (with banana, pear, kiwi, kale, ginger and flaxseed - you should try it), and every now and then I have cryotherapy, which involves standing in a freezing cold chamber set at around -110 degrees Celsius (that's -165 Fahrenheit to Americans). Why? To reduce inflammation, increase cell rejuvenation, improve skin tone and reduce the signs of ageing. Obviously.

How has LA become a mecca for health and wellness? Firstly, it's 72 degrees (that's 22C to Canadians and Europeans) and sunny every day. Of course, it's not exactly the same every day, and it's hotter in summer and cooler in winter, but the climate is pleasant almost all year round. This makes it an outdoor city where people wear light clothing, and where that glorious golden sandy beach stretching down the west side of the city means being beach-body ready.

This is the home of Hollywood, too, which is an industry built on looking good. Plastic surgery plays a big part in keeping time at bay here (you'll look a long way in LA for a forehead that wrinkles, thanks to the Botox revolution of the last decade), but the focus is increasingly on 'optimising yourself'. How can we make ourselves the best we can be, working at peak performance?

Lastly, the internet has democratised information, so we can find virtually anything on it that we need. This isn't unique to LA, but storytelling as a speciality is, and we get much greater access to that storytelling through the internet. If we want to, we can be educated about any aspect of health, from any angle.

Greg Fleishman is the co-founder and president/COO of Foodstirs, a company specialising in organic and reduced sugar home baking mixes, kits and fresh baked goods that endeavours to modernise treats for today's sweet tooth using clean-label products at affordable prices. Actress Sarah Michelle Geller (better known as Buffy the Vampire Slayer) is his co-founder. Greg's experience in the US food industry has given him a unique perspective on how Los Angeles is different. He says:

"Broadly speaking, LA is a major metropolitan area with a high level of education and awareness. The belief that health and longevity are important stems from this dynamic. Another corroborating nuance is that Californians, particularly in Southern California, tend toward vanity, which we all accept as truth. And, in Los Angeles, that is even more amplified: the sun, surf and entertainment industry where looks are very important and the need to always have 'what's new' further supports the uniqueness of this part of the US."

Optimising you

When my mum last came to Los Angeles, she took this photo and sent it to me with a laughing emoji. She thought it was hilarious that vitamin B12 IV drips were being advertised, let alone that anyone would actually want one on a Tuesday afternoon. But she was wrong (sorry, Mum!). Since 2016, IV nutrient therapy - from a hydration to hangover cure, immunity boost, to weight loss - has become increasingly popular in Los Angeles. Use any online search tool and you'll find a plethora of highly-rated options. There are more than 20 options within a five-mile radius of my house.

This is only one piece of the pie.

The term 'biohacking' is regularly used in tech circles around Silicon Valley and Los Angeles. The definition involves biological experimentation to improve the qualities or capabilities of individuals outside a traditional medical or scientific research environment. However, the colloquial use is much wider: someone who enjoys exploring the details of their life or way of living, and wants to stretch their capabilities.

However, Dr Shah is most passionate about overall health and wellness, advising thousands of patients on how to optimise their well-being and extend their lifespan. This culminated in the creation of the company NEXT HEALTH, whose tagline is 'Optimising You'.

NEXT Health offers the latest trends and technologies in health and well-being under one roof. And, let's face it, in a city where people care about their appearance and spend a lot of time wearing very little in warm sunshine, there is a heightened awareness of personal aesthetics and health is an investment.

When you join NEXT HEALTH, baseline tests are run measuring DNA, micronutrients, hormones and general fitness. Based on these, a programme is created which may include some or all of the following:

- Stem cell therapy: seen as the forefront of regenerative medicine, the mesenchymal stem cells are 'adult stem cells' that can make new fat, cartilage and bone cells. Some new parents are medically storing their baby's umbilical cord, which is full of young stem cells, for future use.

- Platelet rich plasma (PRP): a system that takes your blood and separates the components to get the PRP, which is then reinjected into areas to promote collagen growth, regenerate tissue, and smooth and tighten the skin. It's sometimes called the vampire facial.

- IV nutrient drips. Several options can be curated for the individual, whether they're looking for a brain or immunity boost, gut health, more energy, weight loss, or just a glam glow.

- Vitamin shots: for those who don't have time for a drip, these are injected instead of slowly dripped through.

- Cryotherapy: three minutes of extreme cold in a chamber.

- Infrared therapy: stimulating white blood cells to repair damaged tissue and increase collagen production, while triggering endorphins for chronic and acute pain relief.

You can drop in any time you like for check-ups or treatments, which is why the company has outlets in busy areas, such as the Westfield Mall in Century City.

One of the things that struck me about NEXT HEALTH is how health information is gathered, simplified, personalised, and presented on a dashboard in an app.

Most business executives can tell you more about the products and services they manage than they can tell you about their own health. Much of our health is a mystery, left to doctors to decipher and manage, usually pharmaceutically. And we only seek their help when we encounter a problem.

The NEXT HEALTH app allows you to keep track of your health on demand. Do you have any idea what your cholesterol level is, or if your blood pressure is 'normal'? Me neither. So, imagine being able to have all that information - and more - at your fingertips. It makes perfect sense.

Photo credit: NEXT Health

We are only just beginning to use data to improve our overall health. By understanding potential issues ahead of time we can use preventative medicine, which is usually more effective and less invasive. Companies like NEXT HEALTH are leading the way.

Most solutions offered by these companies are not a 'quick fix'; their programmes are built on the premise of creating multiple long-term sustainable habits to improve health.

While some of these 'next generation' services, such as stem cell therapy, are backed by research, they are not approved by the FDA (Food and Drug Administration), so may be a little vanguard for many. Health and nutrition services are certainly becoming more mainstream.

I'm only a step away from being convinced to try one of the IVs, especially after a night on the town. The one thing I have bought into is that we should treat our health better than we treat our tech products - knowing our data and reacting accordingly.

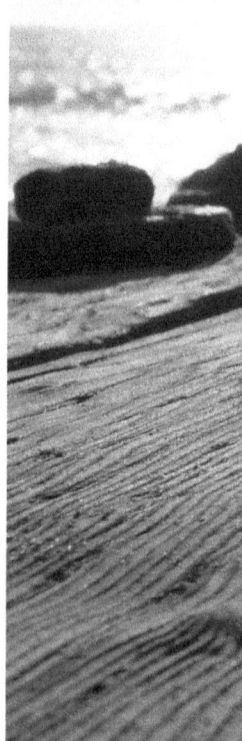

LA's biotech boom

Given Los Angeles' fascination with the advancement of health and well-being, it shouldn't come as a huge surprise that it is one of the biggest biotech hubs in the US.

The biotech industry in LA County generated $42.5 billion in 2018, employing more than 70,000 people. It's one of the only sectors that has grown consistently, even during the recession. But what's more staggering about this is that it's a new industry here in LA, only making its mark in the last decade. Partly thanks to the ambitions of local governments, partly due to the business and venture community, the development of biotech has been a strategic goal for Los Angeles.

Dina Losofsky, LA's Executive Director for Biocom (and, in her words, 'overall cheerleader for all things biotech and all things LA'), helps explain how and why Los Angeles has managed to build such a successful biotech ecosystem in a short amount of time.

1. **Skills and talent**
   Los Angeles has several world-class universities, research institutes and research hospitals. LA County's Life Science industry directly employed 91,713 people in 2018, with average annual earnings of $83,449.

2. **Research centres**
   Dina says "We have world-class research institutions spinning out innovation every day: University of California Los Angeles (UCLA), University of California (USC), and Caltech, in addition to City of Hope, Cedars-Sinai Hospital, and Children's Hospital Los Angeles, as well as many smaller institutions."

3. **Incubators and labs**
   These make it a lot easier for early stage companies as they can share many of the expensive lab services needed to develop their products. They can also benefit from local experience, mentors and other companies in the same space. There are a number popping up, including CNSI on the UCLA campus in Westwood, BioLabs LA BioMed in Torrance and Mothership in downtown Los Angeles.

4. **Location**
   Two of the US's largest biotech hubs were San Diego and Silicon Valley. Located between the two, Los Angeles benefits from proximity to each, making it an easy meeting point.

5. **Funding**
   "The county as a whole receives about $1 billion in National Institutes of Health (NIH) funding from the US Government. This is more NIH funding each year than any other county in California (and California receives more of this funding than any other state in the US)." (NIH funding is commonly used as a measure of the strength of the life science research in a region, since the US government uses this money to fund the most promising technologies and therapies of the future.) There are also a number of venture funds focusing on biotech, including Westlake Village BioPartners' $320 million inaugural fund announced in 2018.

So, how does all of this relate to health? There are a number of examples of how biotech is specifically aiding the improvement of lifestyle.

According to Biocom, Los Angeles' large number of cancer centres, universities, hospitals and clinics is turning research into cures – more clinical trials are conducted in LA County than in California's other life science clusters. Beyond the often profound value to society created by these trials through the medicines themselves, local communities benefit from the investment pouring in to run these trials, including the hiring of staff and contractors, and the recruiting, retention and treatmen of patients.

Dina also highlights a couple of companies that are working to improve patients' lives by helping them manage themselves and their lifestyles.

Canary Health delivers a short online programme for people living with chronic conditions, such as diabetes, to help empower them to take control of their disease management through a set of online tools and peer support.

Moving Analytics developed a comprehensive 12-week, post-heart surgery programme that combines evidence-based guidelines, behavioural science, remote monitoring, and personalised coaching to engage patients to improve their health outcomes instead of solely using rehab centres.

Training
the brain

More and more research is being carried out into how body and mind are linked, from breathing to hypnotherapy to psychedelic drugs (the latter of which is on Gwyneth Paltrow's radar as 'the next big thing'[1]). We train our bodies but our bodies don't stop at the neck - the brain is arguably the most important part of our being.

[1] New York Times 2019 'Gwyneth Paltrow is All Business'

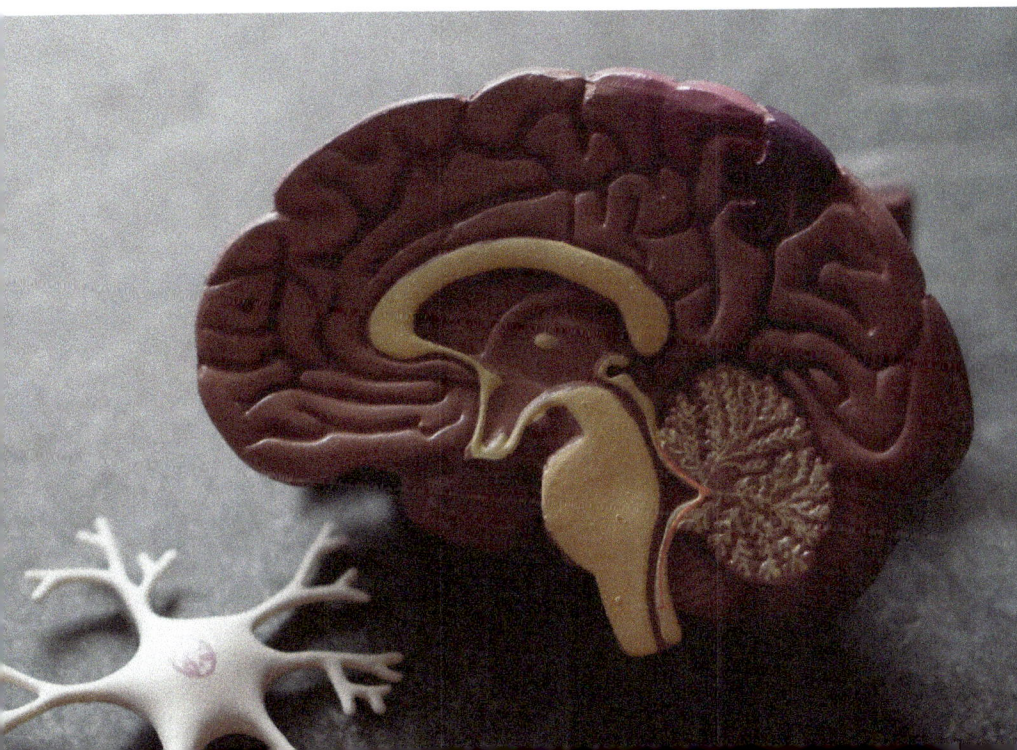

The benefits of meditation are numerous. According to Harvard neuroscientist Sara Lazar, among many of its advantages is that meditation can help slow down ageing, particularly around memory and decision-making. Here are three companies in Los Angeles leading the way:

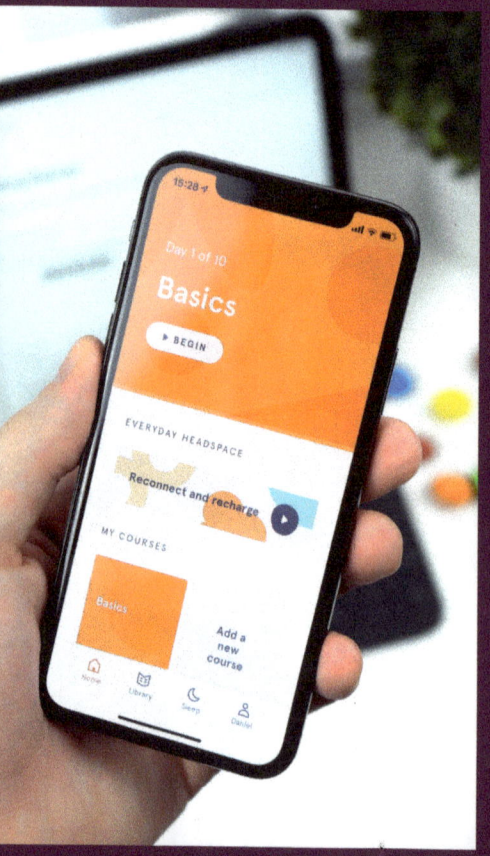

1. **Headspace**

   Andy Puddicombe is a Brit who spent 10 years training in meditation as a Buddhist monk, eventually being ordained at a Tibetan monastery in the Himalayas. When he met Rich Pierson, a stressed-out advertising executive, they swapped meditation advice for business advice - and Headspace was born.

   Originally launched as an events company in 2010, it quickly became clear that people wanted to take Headspace home with them. Rich and the team launched an online service, so that people could use Andy's teachings at home. This morphed into an app of guided meditations, voiced by Andy, which is largely what the business is today. Based in Santa Monica, they have millions of users and claim to be present in 190 countries.

Photo credit: David Young-Wolff, Unplug

2. Unplug Meditation

After a simple three-minute breathing exercise recommended by her mother-in-law, fashion journalist Suze Yalof Schwartz realised how stressed she had been. She needed help. At her relatively new home in Los Angeles, she Googled 'drop-in meditation' but couldn't find one anywhere. She saw the opportunity to create what she had been looking for, and, in 2014, Unplug Meditation was born. Suze claims the Santa Monica studio was the world's first drop-in meditation space.

Suze says doctors regularly send patients to Unplug to help with problems such as infertility, chronic pain and anxiety.

Still very much LA-based, the more-than-60 Unplug teachers often find themselves travelling to teach at pop-ups in New York, help corporations, teach on Oprah cruises, or train teachers internationally, so that they can open their own studios. The business has also expanded with an Unplug book, and an app that focuses on videos of the studio's teachers by time or topic.

3. Esqapes VR

In the basement office of the Screen Actors' Guild building, sitting in a massage chair with a VR headset on, I am at 'Standing Rock', a virtual desert location, watching butterflies and birds gently flutter around a waterfall. This is one of the best LA experiences I have ever had, the epitome of using technology to relax. It works a treat: I'd been racing around all morning, but, after that visit to Standing Rock, my heartbeat was lower and I felt a lot more relaxed and clear-headed.

The reason this experience is unique and so powerful is that it embraces four of the senses: sight, sound, smell, and touch.

With experience at Atari, Yahoo, Disney, and NASA, LA native Micah Jackson created Esqapes "to provide guests with a unique way to relax and take a break from the routines, responsibilities, and daily issues that can cause anxiety and stress. Esqapes is using VR in ways unlike any other company, which is to de-stress and help people relax. With a combination of proprietary software and traditional wellness practices, Esqapes is offering the spa of the future, today!"

Photo credit: Esqapes

Replacing pills
- with a headset?

Virtual reality has had mixed reviews. There was huge hype about how it would change the world, and every person I showed VR to for the first time was blown away by the possibilities. But the hardware hasn't been able to live up to that hype in terms of cost and size, for consumers at least.

However, in some areas, VR has been successful, not least in medicine and healthcare. There are four predominant ways in which VR is having an impact on healthcare:

1. **Education and training**
   Think of it as a flight simulator for doctors. They are able to practice different operations and be tested with unexpected complications without putting a life at risk. This gives doctors a lot more experience before they operate on a real person.

2. **Visualisation**
   Imagine if a doctor could see a 3D scan of an organ and the problem areas close-up just before they operate. Augmented reality may help by layering on additional data and information during operations.

3. **Empathy**
   Maybe seeing life from the perspective of someone with limited or no vision would make a positive change to the way we interact with them. We all want to be heard and have people understand us, now we can place other people in our shoes.

4. **Pain management**
   By placing users in another world simply via a headset, and by using distraction or visualisation content and techniques, pain can be reduced by around 50%.

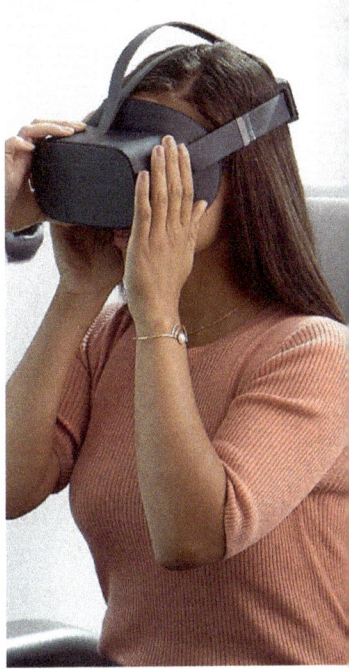

Photo credit: Applied VR

The last of these is already a reality, and a company in Los Angeles is building a VR Pharmacy. So, how does this work? The mind is a powerful thing. By putting on a VR headset and earphones, the patient is taken out of the scenario they are in, tricking the mind into thinking they are elsewhere. As the CEO of Applied VR, Matthew Stoudt, says:

"Through the power of presence, VR creates a significant cognitive load that blocks the pain signals from reaching the pain receptors in the brain."

So far, the technology has been adopted by hospitals - 30,000 patients in more than 250 hospitals and in eight countries globally have used VR to be precise - but there is a future where VR headsets help health at home.

Photo credit: Applied VR

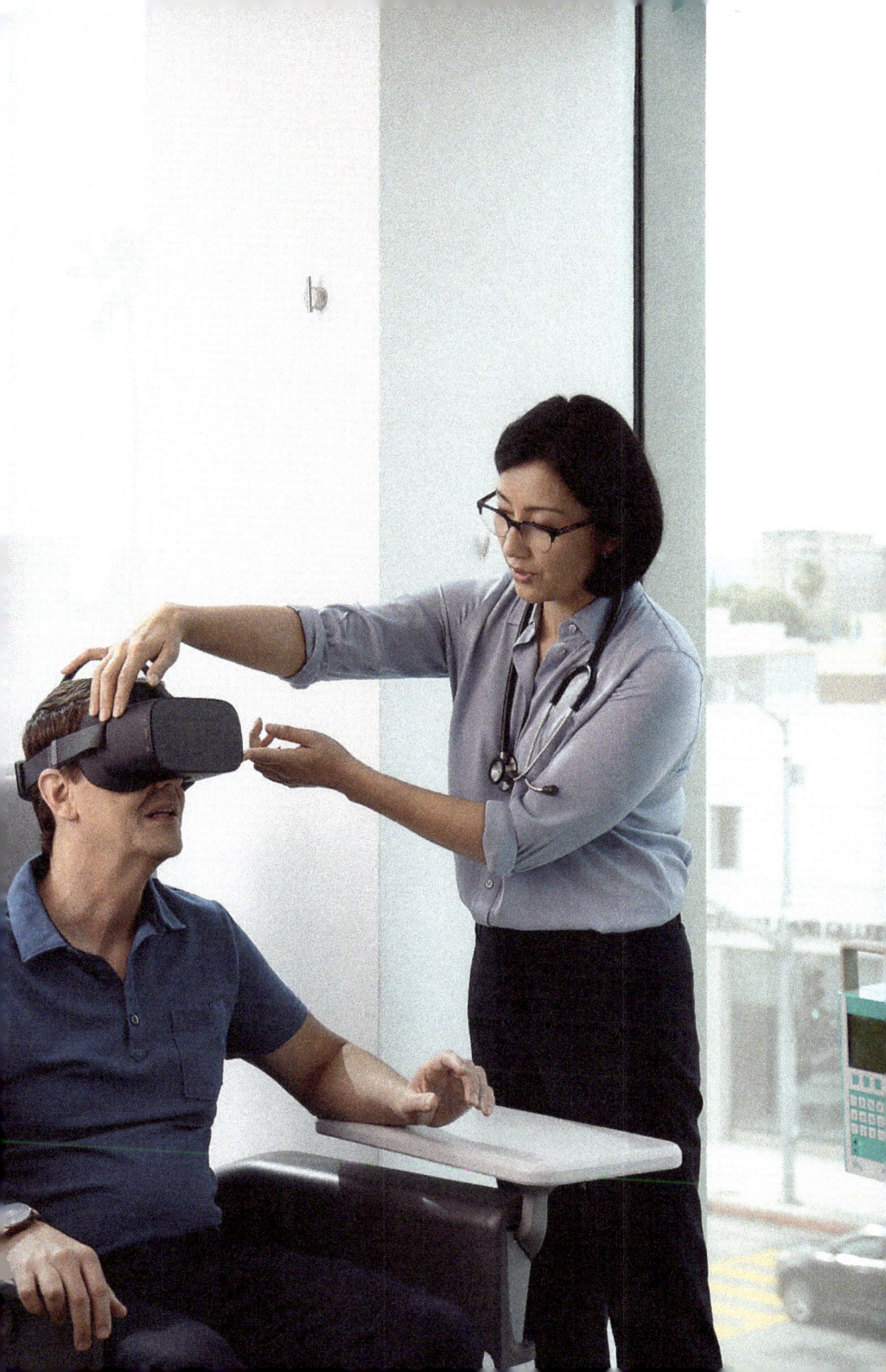

Cannabis

Cannabis is a big deal in Los Angeles. When I arrived in the city four years ago, medical marijuana was already legal and lots of people I met were using it, usually baked in biscuits or edibles and shared among friends. I am a full-on fan and probably use a cannabis-derived product every day, but no, I am not a stoner, I do not smoke, and my THC intake (the psychoactive part of cannabis) is low. Let me explain.

What is Cannabis?

It's complicated. To have a conversation with someone in Los Angeles, here are the basic terms you need to know:

Cannabis, also known as marijuana, is a psychoactive drug from the cannabis plant used for medical or recreational purposes. Cannabis can be used by smoking, vaporising, within food, or as an extract.

There are two major compounds of cannabis:

1. **Tetrahydrocannabinol (THC)** which is the principal psychoactive constituent of cannabis.

2. **Cannabidiol (CBD)** has no psychoactive effect and accounts for up to 40% of the cannabis plant extract. In 2018, clinical research on CBD included preliminary studies of relief from anxiety, movement disorders, and pain.

Hemp is a strain of the cannabis sativa plant species grown specifically for the industrial uses of its derived products. It is one of the fastest growing plants and can be refined into a variety of commercial items, such as paper and clothing. It is often used as the source of CBD.

How is cannabis good for you?

The endocannabinoid system (ECS) is a network of receptors in mammals involved in regulating physiological and cognitive processes including fertility, appetite, pain-sensation, mood, and memory. These physical and cognitive processes are boosted by the cannabinoids in CBD and THC.

Changing public opinion

California was one of the first US states to legalise cannabis, making it available medicinally through the Compassionate Use Act of 1996. By the time I arrived in Los Angeles in 2015, getting a prescription was fairly easy. In fact, on the Venice Beach boardwalk, people were often approached by individuals wearing green T-shirts decorated with cannabis leaves. It was hard NOT to get cannabis. In 2016, there was a vote to make cannabis legal for recreational purposes in California and the Adult Use of Marijuana Act was passed.

By 2018, regulation was in place and stores selling cannabis started opening. They were different to the dispensaries of the past - those random people on the boardwalk. These new outlets were retail stores where the look and feel was entirely different - places you wanted to walk into.

In 2016 stores on the Venice Boardwalk encouraged cheap 'medical' marijuana

"There is a lot of miseducation in the space, and we [the industry] need more brand positioning generally. It's legal, but that's not enough. It's desirable - an experience that creates a good outcome."

Sweetflower is at the higher end of the market in a space that breathes Southern California - which is where their retail outlets are. Sweetflower CEO Tim Dodd is from a media and telecommunications background but knows how to operationalise. He saw the need for superior retail outlets rather than dispensaries. He says Sweetflower is for the cannabis curious.

dosist produces a vape pen for cannabis with a patent on metered control, where the pen gently vibrates to indicate when someone has received a 2.25mg dose. dosist recently opened its own stores on iconic Abbot Kinney in Venice, and West 3rd Street in West Hollywood. Walking in, you could be forgiven for thinking you had entered an Apple store, only with a little less clutter. Clear, clean and predominantly white, these spaces are designed to give the customer the information they need in a relaxing setting. The Abbott Kinney location even has a tranquil garden for customers to relax in.

With legalisation, high end cannabis stores such as dosist can be found on the trendy Abbot Kinney Boulevard

Photos credit: Laure Joliet, dosist

Driving around LA, you'll see dosist billboards among those promoting Hollywood shows and movies. Launched in 2016, the company was named one of Time magazine's 25 best inventions that year as 'cannabis that could replace pills'. The company tagline is 'delivering health and happiness', and it is often seen as promoting plants over pills.

Aside from traditional 'cannabis' companies, CBD companies are booming too. Take Sagely Naturals, which gives 'a fresh approach to feeling better' through CBD-infused products, such as lotions and essential oils. Their two main demographics are millennials looking to manage stress with the Calm & Centered collection and baby boomers dealing with discomfort and exercise-induced inflammation who buy from the Relief & Recovery collection.

With all this high-end retail making the market more accessible, I'm not the only person who's a fan of cannabis. As more research is being done and information made available showing multiple health benefits and few risks (far fewer than drinking alcohol), US opinion is changing. According to Pew Research Center, 62% of Americans are in favour of legalising marijuana. This is up from 30% in 2000. And approval for medical use marijuana rises to 94%[2].

[2] Quinnipiac University national poll 2017

Big business

While many companies in the cannabis industry will talk of their roots being founded in the health aspects of the business, the financial trajectory is also pretty good. When Sagely started their CBD business in 2015, the 2020 CBD market size estimate was $2 billion - more recently, the Brightfield Group revised that estimate to $20 billion by 2022.

Cannabis market valuations vary greatly which is unsurprising given that it's a young industry. Much of the growth will depend on state and federal laws changing, but here are a few valuations from those who know what they are talking about:

- "We believe [US] cannabis can generate gross sales of ~$75 billion by 2030" - Cowen and Company

- "We estimate the total US cannabis market could be just shy of $40 billion in annual sales ... if the uptake in concentrate product is similar to many of the existing legalised states, we believe annual industry sales could reach >$65 billion" - Canaccord Genuity

- "Global medical marijuana market is expected to reach a value of $56 billion by 2025" - Grand View Research

To put the market in context, take a look at cannabis compared to other mainstream products.

Chart source: Packaged Facts, Bloomberg, Nielsen, Euromonitor & Nielsen

It's complicated: the legal stuff

Cannabis is heavily controlled by rules and regulations. In the USA, there are three tiers of regulation:

1. **Federal**
   This governs the country as a whole. Large bodies, such as the US Food and Drug Administration (FDA), are "responsible for protecting the public health by ensuring the safety, efficacy, and security of human and veterinary drugs, biological products, and medical devices; and by ensuring the safety of our nation's food supply, cosmetics, and products that emit radiation."

   Cannabis is not legal at the federal level, but, in late 2018, the 'Farm Bill' was passed in the US, removing industrial hemp from the Control Substance Act and allowing licensed farmers nationwide to grow industrial hemp, from which CBD can be derived.

   Sagely co-founder Kaley Nichol explains: "This helped take CBD to the next level of legitimacy and acceptance by retailers and consumers alike - a big step forward for the cannabis industry." However, it is still not cut and dry; there is a grey area for CBD distribution nationwide since FDA and state-by-state regulation differs.

Photo credit: dosist

2. **State**
Each state can decide to create its own regulation as long as it doesn't contradict federal law. If this seems strange, just think that, if California was a country, it would be the 6th largest economy in the world. Given the vast size of the USA, it makes sense for individual states to have some autonomy.

More than 30 US states have legalised cannabis in some form. State borders are controlled federally, so, even if two adjacent states have legalised cannabis, it is still not legal federally, therefore it may not cross state lines between the two. That means that all cannabis products sold in a particular state must be manufactured in that state. Supply and demand can vary hugely between states. Northern California has some perfect growing conditions known as 'The Emerald Triangle', which means the enormous demand in Los Angeles can be met.

3. **Local**
Individual cities may have their own regulations. For example, Santa Monica is its own city and has some of its own regulations (which can be fairly minor – for example, gardeners may not use a leaf blower!)

It's no wonder cannabis companies often spend millions of dollars on legal advice to remain compliant.

Nothing is ever easy

This is especially so for cannabis-related businesses where legalities are changing every few days. Sweetflower's Tim Dodd says:

"We're doing everything the right way, but it's hard at every turn. Some real estate companies won't lease to cannabis-related businesses as their assets could be seized by the Federal Government; some payroll companies won't work with us; it's been hard to get healthcare benefits for our employees."

The upside for Sweetflower is that, by being first, they're well-placed to expand as the legal and operational frameworks are put in place.

The changes get in the way of the industry, and therefore of us. We know about some of the health benefits of cannabis, but it's widely understood that more testing will give us even more understanding of how cannabis can be used for health and wellness. However, there are serious restrictions around lab testing, which is controlled by the FDA. So, if a lab works with the FDA, it can't work on cannabis.

But Sagely's Kaley Nichol remains optimistic: "Regardless, it is expected that more federally-approved clinical trials of cannabis will now be able to take place over the coming years, which will provide the FDA more clarity and confidence in creating CBD regulations for cosmetics, food, beverages and supplements. This is an incredibly exciting prospect as it will enable wider-scale human studies that can further expand our understanding of CBD and advance research past the preliminary stage. CBD is breaking through the mainstream."

Reaching the market can be tough, since CBD and cannabis companies haven't been able to advertise through traditional media, such as broadcasting and print. Michael Rosenfeld works at CannaVu, a company specifically set up to understand the rules and regulations around cannabis promotion and which has developed the largest source of cannabis-compliant inventory. He says: "The surge in types of CBD and cannabis products entering the market makes it difficult for digital platforms to manage and quickly adapt their policies in light of different compliance requirements in states and federal regulations."

This gives cannabis companies a brand-safe network to advertise on, which is especially useful when most social media platforms won't allow any form of cannabis advertising.

Just to make life even more difficult, another complication that federal limitations have thrown up is that most banking systems won't give cannabis companies accounts. Sweetflower is one of 10 companies accepted on a pilot programme with Credit Union. They're lucky, although they also pay more for the privilege - wire transfers cost around $100 instead of $10. Most companies can't get working capital from banks and suppliers don't work on payment terms, so it's pay for play - a cash-driven industry.

Righting social injustice

Even though medical cannabis was legal in California until 2018, cannabis traded outside this licensing framework was criminalised, meaning that those convicted during this time had a criminal record, and often served time in jail.

Now that cannabis is legal, this causes a dilemma - should someone have a criminal record for something that is now legal? LA County believes not and is in the process of clearing 50,000 of the charges that were brought during that time.

But, for some people, it is already too late. Their criminal record has already affected their employment opportunities and they are feeling the effects. Los Angeles is launching a social equity programme to right this wrong, which will give priority for business licences in the cannabis space to some of those convicted.

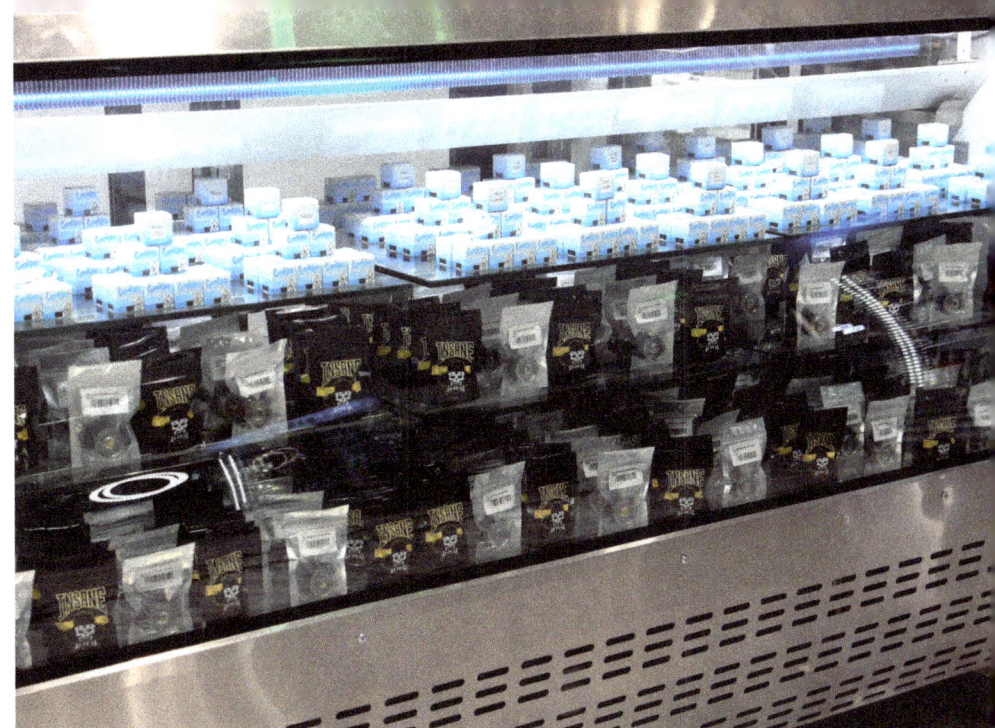

Photo credit: Kathy Hutchins / Shutterstock.com

While this is seen as a good measure socially, helping people who were penalised for something that is now legal, there is concern on both sides. Those receiving licences are concerned that recipients don't have the training and background to create viable, professional businesses. And, for those waiting for the programme to kick off in earnest, this process is taking an exceptionally long time. As the city's Department of Cannabis Regulation notes in an official statement:

"Bringing cannabis above ground is an incredibly complex process, and LA is doing it on an unprecedented scale. Our goal is to do this the right way, not the quick way or the easy way."

Why is Los Angeles a hotbed for CBD and cannabis?

Photo credit: Laure Joliet, dosist

- While most of the growing is done in Northern California, the majority of cannabis companies are based in and around LA. The city is more liberal and there are more people, which makes for a bigger consumer market. Los Angeles City has a population of 3.99m; San Francisco's is 0.88m.

- Perhaps surprisingly, given the concentration of venture capital in Silicon Valley, it has proved easier to raise capital in Los Angeles.

- With Hollywood's roots in storytelling, more brands sit in LA - telling the cannabis story. This is helped by the celebrity angle. dosist has vocal fans from Adam Scott to Jane Fonda. Sagely has an A-list actress as an investor. Sweetflower has released limited collections with artists such as Jenny Lewis.

- There is also a lot of technical innovation, particularly around vaping technology and edibles.

Josh Campbell, President of dosist, says he is going 'California sober' - meaning he's not drinking alcohol, but cannabis is still on the menu.

"In Los Angeles, alcohol is the new cigarettes - people will often judge you for drinking but applaud the cannabis alternative."

TL;DR

- Looks are important in Hollywood, so there is a huge emphasis on health.

- Angelenos are more willing to try new ways to get healthy, which has encouraged startups and advanced trials of new products and services.

- Prevention over cure - there is more awareness of taking care of our bodies to keep in optimal shape for mental and physical wellness.

- Companies are offering comprehensive 'dashboards' for individuals to track their health.

- Health is holistic. More research is being done to understand the relationship between body and mind.

- Previous beliefs are being uprooted and our definition of 'drugs' is changing.

- Non-pharmacological natural remedies are being tested, from cannabis to natural psychedelics through to new technologies, such as VR.

- CBD, a non psychoactive derivative of cannabis plants, is breaking through to the mainstream, and, as more research is done, we can expect to discover more health benefits.

- Cannabis is a huge market and there is still a long way to go in terms of education, law and operationalisation.

Inspiring innovation: from simple family recipe to multi-billion dollar business

GT Dave is revered in Los Angeles. Going to his office in Vernon was a big deal. When building the new office, the team wanted to work out where GT's office should be, so they put him in a crane facing the downtown LA horizon and told him to signal when he had the view he wanted.

That same view can now be seen from his bright white third-floor office, sparse apart from a beautifully crafted desk and a few personally selected art pieces. GT's office is inside a complex where most of GT's Living Foods' manufacturing took place. Until recently, GT tasted every batch of his product, but, as demand continued to boom, it was too much to handle for one person - so, now he has help. Although GT Dave is still personally tasting the equivalent of 1 gallon per day.

His product? Kombucha. A tangy tea, fermented for weeks with a SCOBY (Symbiotic Culture of Bacteria and Yeast), which, according to ancient Eastern tradition, is naturally effervescent and known for supporting gut health, thanks to its living probiotics and active enzymes.

GT Dave and I are around the same age, although he looks younger. He puts that down to his mother's best-ever piece of advice for him when he was just ten years old: use eye cream! I suspect it has more to do with his fantastically healthy lifestyle and regimented work-outs. Either way, whatever he is doing is working.

He was just 15-years-old when he started his company, single-handedly creating a whole new drinks category that is projected to reach USD 5.45 billion by 2025, according to Grand View Research, Inc. But GT Dave doesn't like talking about the numbers, and that's one of the reasons he's so successful - it's all about the product and the effect it has on people's lives.

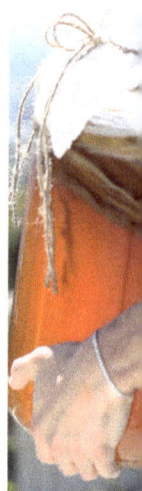

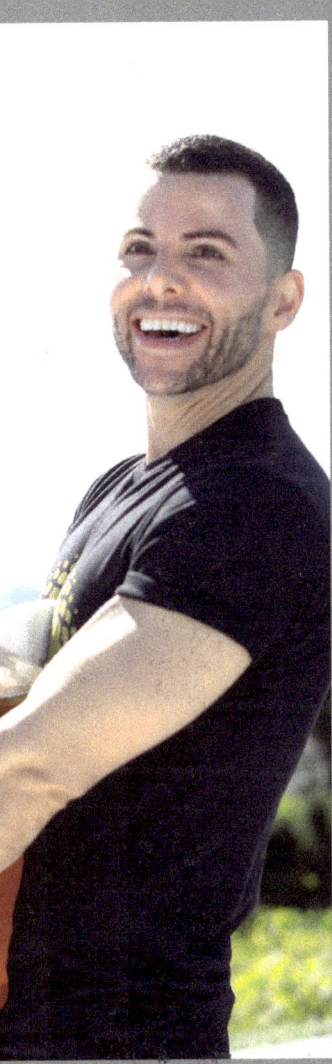

Photo credit: GT Living

The back story is fascinating.

As a teenager, GT Dave changed schools and didn't fit in. Not a typical American male, he worked out but didn't play sport, dated boys not girls, and was teased mercilessly for his vegan lunches. This led to him being bullied and, although he wanted an education, hating school. He decided to study at home and take his high school diploma exams instead of going to high school.

His mother was diagnosed with cancer but, after multiple tests, the doctors couldn't understand how a large cancerous growth had not metastasised. They advised her to carry on doing whatever she'd been doing. She underwent various forms of therapy, including chemo, and realised that, throughout all of this, there was just one thing she was able to hold down and made her feel good. It was a drink she and her husband had been making for a while and drinking every day. That drink was kombucha.

For a while, GT's parents had been giving the drink to friends. Sometimes, they would add extras like cranberry, and their friends kept coming back, saying the drink made them feel good. They shared the Himalayan Scoby (Symbiotic Community of Bacteria and Yeast, effectively a homemade starter mix for kombucha), so their friends could make their own.

Kombucha only has four ingredients, but making it isn't easy. The mixture can't come into contact with certain minerals, otherwise it will go bad. The friends came back, asking GT's parents to sell it to them, and GT Dave suggested they start a business, given demand.

But his father was a lawyer and his mother was recovering from cancer, so they asked their 15-year-old son why he didn't start a business himself – which is exactly what he did.

The timing was perfect, and this unlikely drink became something that gave him a sense of identity and purpose. He called his favourite store in Los Angeles, Erewhon, and asked what it took to get a product in store. It turned out all he needed was a product with a label, a business address and a phone number.

The friend who had given the Daves the initial Himalayan Scoby owned a juice shop and helped with bottles and labels. GT's father helped set up and co-signed the business. GT wore a suit and tie to visit the store and, conscious of his age, positioned himself as a representative of the company rather than the founder, manufacturer and delivery boy.

After trying the kombucha, the store owner said he liked the product and would stock it. He'd need a fresh supply every day. They agreed a price, and work started immediately.

Photo credit: GT Living

Without him realising it, this was the start of GT's incredible journey to creating a brand new drinks category. He focused solely on the business. He didn't have many friends from school and loved what he did. He slept from 4pm to midnight, then bottled, fermented and made deliveries, squeezing in a work-out along the way.

His kombucha was selling well and he managed to get it into four more stores. By then, he had taken over various parts of the family home - the dining room was sealed off as a factory, the garage was used for refrigeration, and he built a shed for supplies, not realising until much later that this set-up wasn't necessarily legal.

Two more significant events took place. GT's brother got cancer and died six months later. And his parents split up. GT's world suddenly looked very different, so he put kombucha at the heart of it - the routine of producing it gave him the peace and comfort he needed.

The threat of the selling of his family home due to his parent's separation created a sense of urgency to move out of the house nd rent an industrial space. He also hired someone to brew by putting an advert in the Spanish language newspaper 'La Opiñon'.

And so it progressed. GT focused on developing the business, getting his drink into Whole Foods Market throughout Southern California, and discovered that he needed to work with their distributor. His kombucha was one of the first 'premium priced' drinks. His mother would do demos in-store and the business was boosted by an article in Los Angeles Magazine entitled 'The Mushroom that Ate LA'.

At various points, GT Dave stalled business development because he wanted to keep control of the quality of his drink and didn't have operations in place for mass production. Until recently, he tested every single batch. Now he tastes a lot, and jokes that he is "probably a little too hands-on for some people here."

He now employs several hundred people. The only investment he ever received was a $10,000 loan from his mother to buy a labelling machine. Until then, all the labels had been applied manually, with a ruler measuring the distance from the bottom, so they aligned exactly on the shelf. GT Dave paid his mother back quickly.

Now kombucha is everywhere: it's on tap in many co-working spaces, and GT Dave curated a full kombucha bar for the music festival Coachella. His brand captures so much that is trendy right now: living well with a focus on health.

GT is an innovator with a strong belief in the health benefits he can help bring to market through other fermented products. A few of my friends swear by a daily spoonful of his COCOYO probiotic yoghurt.

Photo credit: GT Living

Food

The future of food, now

As I gathered food industry leaders together to discuss innovation - founders, CEOs, and executives from several LA-based companies - the conversation around the boardroom table at JP Morgan started very much as I'd expected: Los Angeles is a hub for excellent food. It has easy access to fresh ingredients; the diversity of cultures leads to innovative combinations of flavours, and, as a city, we're very focused on what we eat and on healthy ingredients.

But this theory took a turn thanks to Soylent's CEO, Bryan Crowley, who dramatically unzipped his jacket to reveal a T shirt with the words PRO GMO. I was surprised - surely, we're striving towards organic and clean label, not genetically modified food? The organic food movement is largely only accessible to those of us who can pay a premium for it, Bryan explained, but, if you're not as financially well off, and certainly if you live on Skid Row (LA), the accessibility of nutrition is very different.

With a global population reaching 9.7 billion by 2050, we're never going to be able to feed everyone unless we can enhance technology and growing techniques in an ethical and sustainable way. This explains Soylent's mission 'to make complete, sustainable nutrition accessible, appealing, and affordable to all'. The company has engineered all the necessary attributes to a complete meal - proteins, carbs, fats, vitamins, and minerals - and delivers them to you as a drink, a powder, or a snack bar. It certainly gave us a different, and valid, point of view.

Food

One of the key eating trends in LA is 'natural food' – grown rather than manufactured or slaughtered. In 2005, a book called *The China Study* was published that seemed to have a particular impact on Los Angeles. It demonstrated links between the consumption of animal products and chronic diseases. Equally, it showed that people who had a predominantly plant-based diet would escape (or could at least reduce the risk of) chronic disease. Being vegan became cool again – it's good for us as individuals *and* it's good for the planet.

LA's grocery shops are stocked with plant-based products, as well as plenty of gluten-free and dairy-free foods. The city is the home of the iconic Erewhon grocery shop, whose mission is to make healthy, pure, nutrient-rich foods and products available to all, and to inspire people to eat better, eat less and live longer. They work directly with suppliers and impose stringent regulations on everything you see on their shelves. This, of course, is reflected in their pricing.

Thrive has a similar ethos and delivers to the door. On many restaurant menus, you can read the names of the farms that produced the ingredients. There's more and more transparency around what is in our food.

When I suggest the idea that LA creates trends to Greg Fleischman, Co-Founder & President/COO, Foodstirs Junk-Free Bakery and a US food industry veteran, he corrects me.

"Los Angeles is good at formalising and legitimising trends. It doesn't necessarily create them - Austin, San Diego, Boulder and other 'leading edge' cities often start micro trends which include pressed juice, CBD and even cold-brew coffee. But LA has scale for mass consumption; it has 'early-adopter-friendly' stores and it has celebrities to drive critical, high impact awareness".

Photo credit: Every Table

One of the first things that struck me when I arrived in the US was how different service is here compared to in Europe. In the US, good service is focused on efficiency and ensuring you have what you need, even if that means a waiter interrupting a conversation or clearing plates away while a fellow diner is still eating. Great service means you are served efficiently and can then leave the restaurant to pursue other activities. In other parts of the world, eating is the activity. Dining in the States can be a steep learning curve for foreigners, including me.

This 'efficiency' of eating is reflected in many homes in the US. Sam Polk, of Everytable, a grab-and-go restaurant making healthy food affordable and accessible for all, has an interesting theory that helps to explain this - and how it's starting to change.

Sam believes our approach to food is the result of a failed experiment. His theory is that, in the 1950s, women were at home cooking, then suddenly there was a shift to processed food driven by shelf-life stability which also made it cheaper. This coincided with women joining the workforce in huge numbers in the '80s and '90s, so the demand for faster, easier food grew sharply.

It was a successful business model, but nobody realised that the ingredients used in this type of food could be so damaging, directly resulting in high levels of obesity, diabetes, and heart disease. Now, maybe because of that, many of us are more aware of the food we put into our bodies.

Location, location, location

There is a trend towards transparency when it comes to ingredients, and we hear more and more about 'clean label' - not just organic or non-gmo (genetically modified organism). Consumers take note of ingredients, and this is forcing companies to think about what goes into their food. This trend is taking hold in the most surprising places too - the fast food chain Taco Bell now only uses organic ingredients. It may be too late for some old-established brands to change people's perceptions of them, even if they have improved their ingredients. Time will tell.

Photo credit: Soylent

Bryan Crowley of Soylent pushes back against some aspects of the "clean label movement" and the idea that fewer ingredients is always better. As an example, Soylent lists all of our 26 vitamins and minerals and the percentage of each based on the RDIs (recommended daily intake), so you know exactly what you are getting. However, he points out that, if you think about a simple food, like a mango, and list out all of the nutrients and compounds in the fruit, then the label would no longer be simple and short. Scientific names of vitamins and minerals are not seen as "clean," but they do provide the nutrients your body needs.

Fresh fruit and vegetables are plentiful as Los Angeles is uniquely positioned within a couple of hours' drive of two of the most prominent growing areas in the country: the Central and Imperial Valleys.

Central Valley covers 11% of California and provides half of the fruit, vegetables and nuts supplied to the entire USA. This proximity is perfect for catering and restaurants. Tara Maxey, co-founder of Heirloom LA, a prominent catering company, says:

"We have incredible accessibility to ingredients and we get ingredients directly delivered to us. We can get incredible local ingredients, sometimes picked that morning."

Photo credit: Heirloom LA

Tara Maxey of Heirloom LA checking out Apricot Lane Farms, a potential supplier.

Heirloom LA doesn't always source from certified organic farmers. This is for very valid reasons: even though these farmers follow the same processes, it is a tedious, long, and expensive process to be awarded organic certification. Tara explains, "we source locally and purchase from many of our farmers directly. I am able to visit their farms and see that they are using, not just organic practices, but regenerative and sometimes even biodynamic practices as well. The quality of their soil is their livelihood since they are growing for flavour rather than quantity. Certified organic farming allows for sprays, but we support farmers who do not use any sprays. Rather, they use crop rotation and biodiversity to keep their crops healthy. Our chosen farmers are, essentially, soil farmers."

Clearly not every ingredient needed to produce food can be grown in LA, but again the city comes up trumps; the ports of Los Angeles and Long Beach give easy access for imports from South America and Asia.

Photo credit: Heirloom LA

Some companies, such as Foodstirs Junk-Free Bakery™, believe that local is limiting. California is a wealthy place; perhaps it should be supporting global economies. For these companies, fair trade means treating the communities that supply their ingredients equitably, so they subsidise the workers and their children by providing better working conditions, libraries, access to healthcare and other programmes. Galitl Hadari Laibow, the co-founder and CEO of Foodstirs, says:

"When we talk about local, it's also about stepping outside our local and actually helping other economies grow and prosper."

Eating out in LA

Photo credit: Lippe Oosterhof

Name one ethnic cuisine that can't be found in Los Angeles. You'll struggle! With the vast diversity in population that makes up LA comes a vast diversity of food. A rich landscape includes high-end restaurants run by well-known chefs, good local eateries, food trucks and sidewalk vendors, all of them selling tasty food.

LA's chefs specialise in feeding a specific community exactly where they are and at a relevant price point according to Eater LA's Farley Elliott, author of *Los Angeles Street Food: A History from Tamaleros to Taco Trucks*.

Why 'exactly where they are'? Because traffic in LA can be awful, so people tend to stay in the area where they live and work.

"Inexpensive, flavourful food. That's LA's Wheelhouse."

Farley Elliott, Eater LA

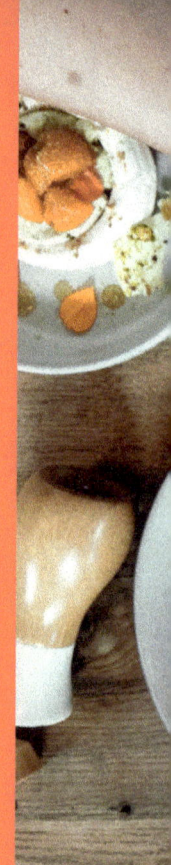

But the roads that produced all this traffic also helped to develop a new food culture. As the highways were built in the 1950s, the drive thru was created. McDonalds is seen as the restaurant that brought the 'drive in' to fame, but LA's iconic In N Out is credited with being the country's very first drive thru. The cost of land to accommodate a restaurant and car park was steep, so canny executives developed a system where cars drove through rather than parked up, saving them the vast cost of providing a car park. In that first drive thru, they used an intercom system not that different from the ones in use today.

In N Out has many celebrity fans: Gigi Hadid popped in while shooting her Vogue cover video, and Aziz Ansari was there in his tux straight after the Golden Globes, celebrating his win for 'Master of None'. As with any stylish Los Angeles venue, there's more here than meets the eye - In N Out has a secret menu (my friends swear by the Animal-style burger, or, if they're ravenous, they'll upgrade the double double to a 3×3).

Another famous spot, seen in the movie La La Land, is Grand Central Market, which recently celebrated its centenary. It was originally built for the white, affluent neighbourhood of Bunker Hill, with customers taking the Angels Flight tramway up and down the hill. However, as people moved out to the suburbs after WWII, the area was almost deserted, giving way to cheaper rents and a less well-off crowd.

When the 2008 recession hit, many places in the market closed down. With downtown LA's regeneration in the last decade, the market was revamped into what it is today - a buzzing spot with a mix of legacy and trendy new vendors. It was named by Bon Appétit as one of the best new restaurants in the US in 2014.

Many of the hot new restaurants of recent years have opened on the same side of town as Grand Central - the east side. Some say this movement was started by New York Chef David Chang, who bought a home in Los Feliz and wanted his restaurant nearby. But there are also practical reasons why this area has attracted so many new high-end places: the east side has more space, the rents are cheaper, and it's more diverse.

The west side of the city is more expensive, with sprawling estates of large houses. Wealthy areas aren't always the best for restaurants - somewhere with a higher population density can generate lots more traffic.

Areas with stringent local regulations, such as Santa Monica, ask business owners to jump through more hoops.

Los Angeles' restaurant scene is different to New York's and other metropolitan areas. It's rare to find a high-end tasting menu. More often, you will find excellent quality food frequently served family style, delivered from the kitchen as it is made, often in an outdoor seating environment.

There is one man who knows this scene better than anyone, and that's Jonathan Gold. For four decades, the LA Times food critic traversed the city discovering all kinds of dining experiences and often enjoyed hole-in-the-wall restaurants as much as - if not more than - Michelin-starred menus.

Jonathan Gold told LA Weekly in 1998:

"For a while in my early 20s, I had only one clearly articulated ambition: to eat at least once at every restaurant on Pico Boulevard, starting with the fried yucca dish served at a pupuseria near the downtown end and working methodically westward toward the chili fries at Tom's No. 5 near the beach. It seemed a reasonable enough alternative to graduate school."

Jonathan got under the skin of the city. His columns went beyond food, embracing the owners and cultures of restaurants, raising awareness of food on so many levels. The 2015 movie 'City of Gold' immortalises his journey and helps reveal the city to those who don't know it.

Until his death in 2018, Jonathan Gold was such an icon in his field that he could change the fate of a restaurant simply by giving it a good review.

Now restaurant discovery is based on three factors:

1. Traditional publishing sources, such as Eater LA and the newer Infatuation

2. Word-of-mouth

3. Social media

Some Los Angeles restaurants are exploiting the latter, particularly by leveraging visuals with Instagram. It's Hollywood's DNA emerging in the form of storytelling through images.

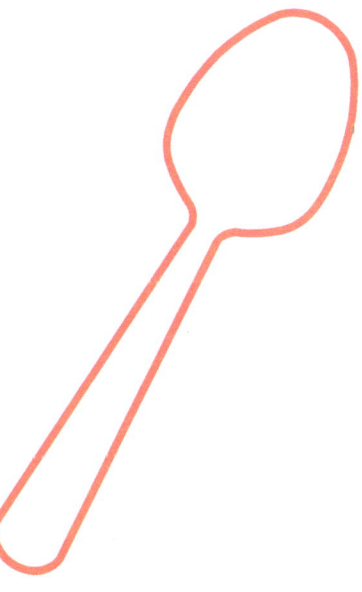

Take @teddysredtacos, which started as a pop-up then moved to a food truck, exploded on Instagram (they have 90k followers), and now has a permanent spot just off the popular Venice boardwalk. Or @tacoselvenado, which is making the most of LA's new fascination with Tijuana-style tacos and has garnered 117k followers on Instagram. Or @HowlinRays, a Nashville-style hot chicken take-out spot in Chinatown's Far East Plaza, which has 147k Instagram followers.

Photo credit: Instagram, @teddysredtacos

Photo credit: Instagram, @tacoselvenado

Kogi BBQ is a master of Twitter, using the medium to let its 148k followers know where the Korean BBQ taco truck will be. Yes, that's Korean BBQ tacos, with the short rib taco being the most popular. One thing LA does better than most cities is leverage its diversity to further creativity in all sectors. Filipino Lasa in Chinatown, for example, makes a Filipino spaghetti with pancit canton noodles, sweet tomato sauce, and aged cheddar. They've also made their twist on cacio e pepe.

Photo credit: Instagram, @HowlinRays

Farley Elliott says:

"We don't use the word fusion anymore; it's just endemic of cooking in Los Angeles."

The problem with Angelenos and ice cream

Many Americans have an affinity with ice cream - it's the birthplace of Häagen-Dazs and Ben & Jerry's, after all. The problem for Angelenos is that, although they love ice cream, it is the antithesis of healthy. For some, this is a serious dilemma. For a few, it's proven to be an opportunity to create something new.

Halo Top

Justin Wolverton was a lawyer who played around with a few recipes to reduce his intake of sugar and carbohydrates. He found a winning combination that kept the texture and taste of ice cream but significantly reduced the calories. He quit his job and racked up credit card debt to kick off the business. After he perfected the recipe he managed to get shelf space at several Los Angeles supermarkets, including Sprouts and Erewhon.

In July 2017, Halo Top became America's best-selling ice cream pint in grocery stores. They now have more than 20 flavours and three stand-alone 'scoop shops' in LA, plus a thriving social media profile with more than 700k Instagram followers.

Halo Top vs leading brands

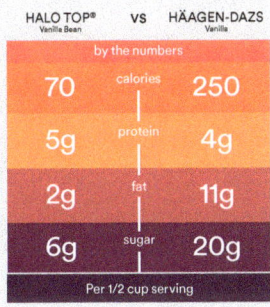
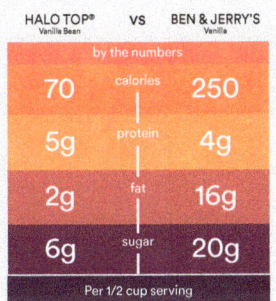
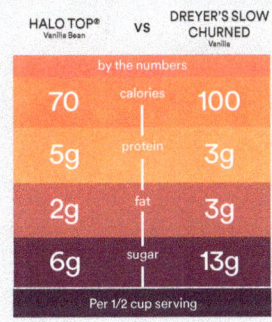

	HALO TOP® Vanilla Bean	HÄAGEN-DAZS Vanilla	HALO TOP® Vanilla Bean	BEN & JERRY'S Vanilla	HALO TOP® Vanilla Bean	DREYER'S SLOW CHURNED Vanilla
calories	70	250	70	250	70	100
protein	5g	4g	5g	4g	5g	3g
fat	2g	11g	2g	16g	2g	3g
sugar	6g	20g	6g	20g	6g	13g
	Per 1/2 cup serving		Per 1/2 cup serving		Per 1/2 cup serving	

Snow Monkey

As a college athlete, Rachel Geicke tracked her macro nutrients and realised that the foods she loved didn't love her back. She explains: "Every time [I] indulged in ice cream, it just threw things off and [I] felt guilty." So, Rachel developed a frozen blend using only superfoods of fruits and seeds, which are high in protein, vegan and paleo.

After graduating from college, Rachel raised money on Kickstarter, reaching her goal in just four days, which got her business started. Two years later, it's not just Angelenos who have embraced the frozen treat; Snow Monkey is now in 100 stores in 28 states. Rachel says: "I grew up in Hong Kong and, when I moved to the States, [it] became so evident to me that Americans have this deep emotional connection to ice cream. I definitely had it too."

Photo credit: Instagram, @EatSnowMonkey

Technology and food - it's not what you think

1. Education and access to information

With easy access to information, people around the globe can educate themselves about food. From artisanal producers and farmers to industry commentators, influencers, and celebrities snapping photos of their food, we see more information about food than ever before.
No more so than Tastemade, the Santa Monica-based 'global, digital food, and travel network for millennials that lets users explore cuisine from around the world through a mix of original content and user-submitted videos.'

COO Geraldine Martin Coppola explains: "The rise of mobile and social platforms and the connectivity of people is enabling information about food and education in a way that could never have happened before. And when consumers have that information then they can take action in terms of what they consume. I think we can also inspire people to do things. We talk a lot about health but food is also just fun, and part of what technology and digital content can do is enable people to share food. Something like 65 or 70% of younger people just post images of [the] food they eat, which has enabled food to become a kind of social currency."

2. The Netflix effect on consumer spending

Since Netflix and chill became household words, another trend has taken hold: home delivery of food through third parties, such as Uber Eats, Postmates, and DoorDash. Consumers now have easy access to great screen content and can get hot, fresh food delivered to their door - why would you ever go out?

Meredith Sandland, COO of Kitchen United, puts this into perspective in her blog: "29% of millennials order restaurant delivery each week. 80% of those aged 18-34 have ordered restaurant delivery at some time. An average millennial spends $1,000 (nearly 25%) less each year on groceries for preparation at home than someone their same age just 10 years ago. That portion of their budget is flowing to… you guessed it, delivery."

As an industry veteran with years of experience as a Taco Bell executive, Meredith knows what she's talking about. Kitchen United is a 'virtual restaurant' housing several restaurant brands - some new and independent, some better known - offering full support services from handling online ordering through to dishwashing. This effectively strips out non-essential costs, so consumers are getting great value for money.

The other thing to note about Kitchen United is that it understands it has another 'customer' it needs to cater for - the delivery drivers. So, the company offers 15 minutes' free parking, free tea, coffee, and water, plus use of the restrooms.

This is becoming such a hot trend that Travis Kalanick, the founder of Uber, is building a similar business, Cloud Kitchens, with its HQ in LA.

3. Moving from bricks and mortar to e-commerce

"70% of Americans use smartphones to order food and that shift is only accelerating," says Alex Canter, founder of Ordermark.

"The restaurant industry is in the early stages of moving from brick and mortar to e-commerce and online ordering."

As the fourth generation operator of the world-famous Canter's Deli in Los Angeles, Alex looked at technologies that would help his family's restaurant adapt to new consumer behaviors and grow. He listed with order delivery sites Eat24 and Grubhub, which improved revenues dramatically. Over time, he found that the more online ordering services he added, the more revenue grew. In fact, revenue increased by 30% within five years by using order out service. Their restaurant is not alone.

Delivery companies are becoming more prolific, varying in success by geography (GrubHub may dominate in some areas, Doordash in others) as well as specialism ('Slice' caters purely for pizza-related delivery, and 'Caviar' for high-end restaurants). Each delivery company has its own processes and technology, sometimes including hardware, which can create operational challenges for restaurants.

Ordermark simplifies things for restaurants by consolidating orders from all of these delivery online ordering services. Providing a single tablet and printer for restaurants to manage orders from multiple ordering services enables restaurants to work with a wide range of online ordering services.

Alex tells me that one chain, Johnny Rockets, increased its delivery revenues six-fold in the first six months of using this system.

Focused on holistic solutions for restaurants, Ordermark is already finding itself a trove of useful data. They're using that to help restaurants improve their businesses, from choosing the best photos to menu planning and display, and letting them know when new online ordering services join the system.

"Restaurants of the future will optimise for convenience OR experience; there's going to be a division between the two. We want to help those who are focusing on convenience by focusing on a holistic solution that allows restaurants to control the whole operation by giving them the tools they need." - says Alex Canter

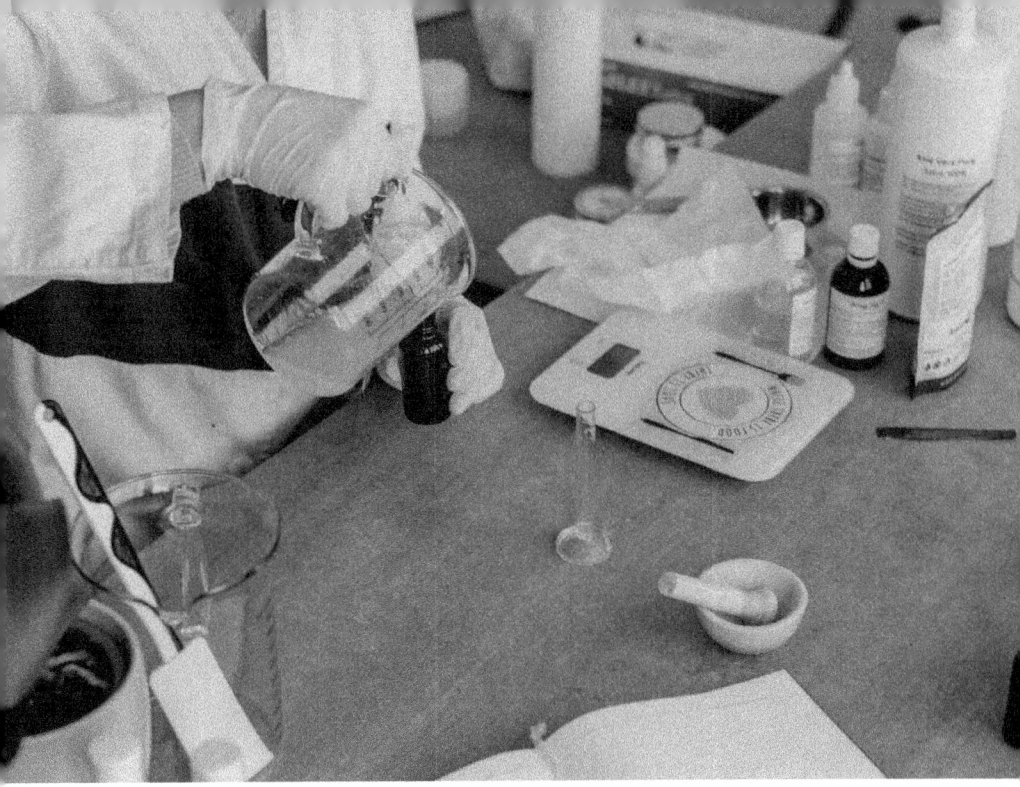

4. Scientific advances in lab-grown food

One person who has a lot to say about this is Bryan Crowley at Soylent: "I believe cellular or clean protein is the next thing. You've got Impossible Foods [in the Bay Area], you've got Beyond Meat [in LA], and both companies are on a mission to give people familiar, delicious foods that have always been animal based, but now with plants. These science-based solutions encourage vegetarians, flexitarians, and meat-eaters alike to indulge without as many trade-offs to their health or to the planet."

Bryan is not alone in understanding the need to look at non-traditional solutions to feed the growing population - and soon.

He points out that, although it 'creeps some people out', we need to understand how we can grow food in a lab. He is also pro-science and therefore pro-GMO, noting that science supports it and we need to make safe and sustainable changes to our crops in order to meet demand.

"Consumer education around this topic is critical, especially when, for 15 years, everyone's been saying clean label, clean label, clean label."

Bryan says organic and clean label can be good for us, but is not widely accessible or affordable, so more research must be done into cellular nutrition/clean protein in order to make foods that are nutritious, sustainable for the future of the planet, and accessible for those whose budgets don't stretch far enough.

Micro food innovator: the street vendor

Sometimes, on the way home from the office, I stop at a small fruit stand near my house to pick up some fresh mango or pineapple, already cut and prepared. Some (crazy!) people add the spicy powder that's offered up too. Occasionally, I've been known to grab a street-side taco. Both are delicious. I love street vendors here, but hadn't stopped to think much about them until I started writing this book.

There are estimated to be more than 50,000 street vendors in Los Angeles, around 10,000 of them selling food. In 2015, a report[1] estimated the total street vending market in LA to be $504 million, with food vendors representing more than $100 million of that sum. This number may seem unsurprising given the diversity of a city that celebrates street food and entrepreneurship. However, until 2017, street vending was a criminal activity: vendors could be fined, have their equipment confiscated, or even be deported.

In 2019, after a decade-long campaign by street vendors culminating in a march on LA's town hall, street vending was finally made legal - a move celebrated by many, as it allows self-employment, taxes, and more safety and regulation.

[1] Economic Round Table Sidewalk Stimulus 2015

Ask the experts: why is food innovation thriving in LA?

"Silicon Valley and VC investment has totally changed the funding model for food and beverage start-ups. 20 years ago, you would never get an investor to sit down, taste your product, and say, 'Wow, look at these trends. Here's $2 million seed right now'. Soylent has been a catalyst for a number of LA-based new food and beverage companies, as they were able to secure funding using our model as an example. As long as there is access to capital, you're going to continue to see a lot of great innovation." Bryan Crowley, CEO, Soylent

"Los Angeles is known for doing things on a bigger level in terms of consumer products. High spend but better brand visibility, celebrity partnerships and market awareness. But this sometimes means bigger spend and higher burn rate - which, in turn, means more need for outside capital. If the margin profile of the business is strong, the operator can quickly burn their way to profitability, which reduces the risk in the investment." Filipp Chebotarev, Chief Operating Officer, Cambridgespg.com

"The infrastructure is very strong here [in LA]. You have density of grocery stores like nowhere else, and a population - with the number of people here - close to the group that represents a market for you. I personally believe that LA is the center of the universe as far as food is concerned." Michel Algazi, Co-Founder, LA Prep (now Amped Kitchens) and CEO Food Centricity

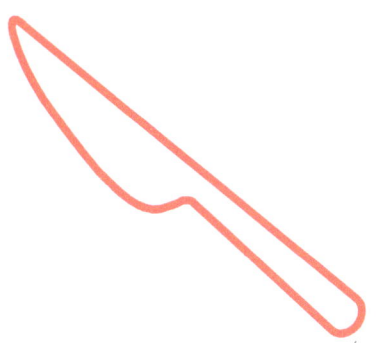

"In LA, there is the ability to be scrappier. In New York, you simply don't have the space to do what I did [creating a business in my home kitchen and garage] - where would you sleep? There is an attitude that comes with the weather [in LA], which gives the ability to do things you couldn't in other climates - I was able to store material outside without it freezing. And, being so close to nature – the oceans, hills, canyons – there's an innate sense of wellness that encourages a healthier lifestyle, making the people here very open to innovate or to try new food, beverages, and exercise trends." GT Dave, Founder, GT's Living Foods

"It's a great place to find a mix of both creative and tech talent. Because I think it's now easy to get engineers to come down from Silicon Valley and work here because there's enough of an ecosystem of companies and they want the lifestyle that they can't get up north. You also have this amazing kind of creative marketing core and that didn't necessarily exist before. So, I think it depends on the type of companies you're trying to create. I think it's just been a great place to have that mix of art and science that makes for great kinds of companies for innovation, especially in the early days where you want to have that." Geraldine Martin Coppola, COO, Tastemade

Sweetgreen

Sweetgreen is no ordinary salad bar. The three founders met and launched their first restaurant while at college in Washington DC. Eleven years later, the company has a valuation of more than $1 billion and is expected to IPO in the near future. It has made Los Angeles its HQ, manages almost 100 locations in eight states, and has 3,500 team members.

Given the number of salad bars in existence, you could be excused for thinking that there was no room for innovation in this sector. But you'd be wrong. Sweetgreen has managed to tap into several themes that resonate with their customers, and the founders have managed to bring these themes to life in an authentic way.

Photo credit: Sweetgreen

They believe in real, sustainable food
Everything is made from scratch in their kitchens. Food is seasonal and sourced locally where possible. They design around sustainability, including sourcing, store design, and waste management. They have a dedicated team that continuously seeks out and researches the latest welfare standards, and they work directly with more than 150 farmers across the country.

Localise where possible
While there is a Sweetgreen style, each store has its own feel based on the culture of the locality. They think of this as their retail merchandising store front and add touches that make each place unique, including the music that is played. In each store, there is a clearly visible list of where farm ingredients are sourced.

Use of technology
They have almost 100 stores and more than 1 million users of their app. That's 11,000 per store, something which is unheard of (Starbucks has around 815). They also partner with forward-thinking companies, such as Ripe. io, which is creating the blockchain for food to improve industry goals for sustainability, spoilage reduction, safety, nutrition and quality.

Connecting the physical and the digital

They put a lot of focus on their digital brand and connecting with the physical brand. Until recently, online orders had to be picked up in-store as the company wanted people to have a physical touch-point. Now the brand has grown, they no longer see this as a necessity.

They have fun with partnerships

As part of their food education in schools programme, they approached Kendrick Lamar, who also plays at their music festivals, to create a salad. Their theory was that this would promote healthy food, and any profits from the salad would go directly into the education programme. 'Beets don't kale my vibe' became the most popular salad that season.

They do some good

Sweetgreen works with several non-profits, including FoodCorps (education in schools), Los Angeles Food Policy Council (advocating for healthy, affordable, fair, and sustainable food for all), and, with every store opening, they partner with a local organisation to whom they donate 100% of opening day profits.

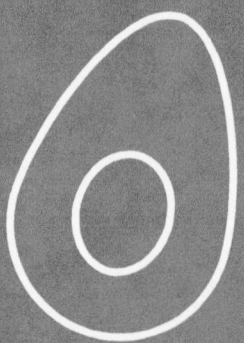

Photo credit: Sweetgreen

> "Our original headquarters was in DC but we're all based in LA now. We relocated because most of our growth is coming from here, our suppliers are mostly here, and we wanted to be on the front lines."
>
> Jonathan Neman, Co-Founder and CEO, Sweetgreen

Making food fair

Los Angeles is one of the most diverse cities in the world, but inequality still exists here. As Sam Polk, CEO of Everytable, writes on his LinkedIn profile: "Healthy food is a human right. But $9 green juices and $12 salads make healthy food a luxury most people can't afford. In fact, many communities in the US have so little access to healthy, affordable food they're called 'food deserts'. These communities experience high rates of obesity, diabetes, and stress."

Everytable is a mission-driven grab-and-go restaurant making healthy food affordable and accessible for all. It has a two-tier pricing approach: wealthy areas pay slightly inflated rates which allows the company to sell the same fresh nutritious meals at discounted rates in food deserts.

The local city didn't agree with his definition of 'maintenance' and issued a citation for gardening without a permit. After a lengthy battle, Ron stuck to his guns in the strong belief that he and his neighbours should be able to grow fresh produce - and he got the law changed.

Now LA County offers tax breaks to owners of vacant land if it is used for urban farming. It's part of the California Urban Agriculture Incentive Zones (UAIZ) Act to encourage local communities to start gardens and reap the rewards. Owners of plots up to three acres can get significant tax breaks if they use or lease the land for agricultural purposes.

The Everytable model is one of the most exciting experiments of food democracy in L.A. and in America.

–LA TIMES–

Hank's Mini Market

The Los Angeles Food Policy Council (LAFPC) has launched a Healthy Neighborhood Market Network programme to empower small business owners in low-income neighbourhoods to bring good food to their communities. They work directly with store owners to help revitalise their shop and source healthy food through collectives to stimulate community vitality and economic development.

One such store in the Hyde Park neighbourhood is Hank's Mini Market run by Kelli Jackson, daughter of the store's founder. The store has been part of the community for more than 20 years: Kelli respected what her parents had created but felt she could do more. She enrolled in the LAFPC's programme, which offers training for local shop owners in everything from business development to marketing and pricing strategy. In some cases, they also help with complete transformations. This was one of those cases.

LAFPC also asked Sweetgreen to get involved. Rather than just write a cheque, their team used their expertise to help Kelli with everything from design to sourcing, pricing strategy and financial planning. Rather than taking over, they helped Kelli realise her own vision. It was an intense process, during which true friendships were forged.

As well as gaining new friends, Hank's Mini Market grew revenue by more than 300% from 2017 to 2018.

Hank's Mini Market before and after

Photo credit: LAFPC

TL;DR

- Humans have an affinity with food. It's something that brings us all together, irrespective of race, creed, or colour. And the skills emerging from Hollywood mean Los Angeles can curate and tell these stories to the world.

- LA is uniquely positioned and has access to incredible local ingredients from an almost perfect growing environment, with imports coming from the South and East through local ports.

- 'Organic', 'clean label', 'plant-based', 'gluten-free', 'dairy-free': LA is at the vanguard of these health-focused trends.

- So many cultures in one small area leads to more flavours and experimentation, creativity, and a willingness to take more risks. Chefs with imagination and flair are driving the innovation of taste in their kitchens every day.

- We're going to see more traditional restaurants embrace delivery services, e-commerce, and the rise of 'virtual restaurants' designed around delivery services take 'ready-made' food to a whole new level. And consumers won't be able to tell the difference.

- Food is an ancient industry, but there is still room for growth, as demonstrated by GT Dave, the king of kombucha.

- The future of food is rosy for those who can afford the more expensive organic, clean label. However, there is still a big gap and work to be done for those at the other end of the scale. For the sake of the growing global population and depleting resources, we need science and technology to come together to offer non-traditional solutions.

Transport

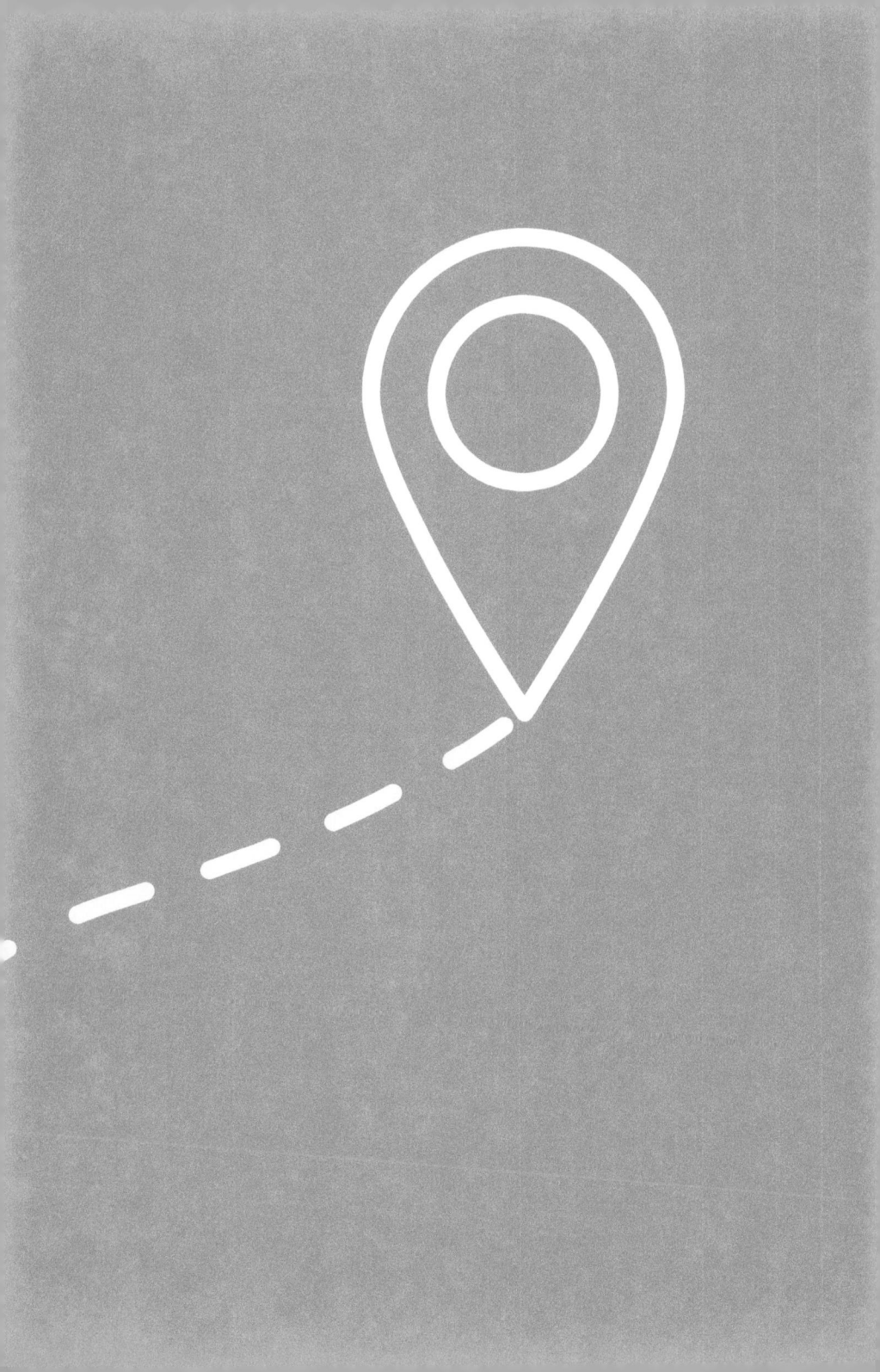

Navigating Los Angeles and beyond

LA is not like other cities. It's not like London, Paris, or New York where you can tick off the sights you want to see. There is no city centre: it's a city of cities. Think of it as a mass of cities that have run into each other, forming a giant metropolis.

Aside from the City of Los Angeles, LA County comprises 87 other cities, including West Hollywood, Santa Monica, and Beverly Hills. The whole area is colloquially known as LA.

There are a few densely developed areas, such as downtown LA, but high-rise is quite rare: most areas consist of single-storey bungalow homes surrounded by towering palm trees.

There are a few reasons for this decentralised LA sprawl. Following the attack on Pearl Harbor, Los Angeles was seen as a potential target, so a blackout of Downtown LA (DTLA) was ordered. Dark streets at night attracted unwanted types, and a feeling of unsafety led to families moving out of the city to the suburbs, mostly towards the west, nearer the sea. With the completion of the Metropolitan Los Angeles Freeways in 1950, which connected different neighbourhoods, there was less need for a centralised city. In fact, it's only in the last 20 years that DTLA has re-established itself as a major city, undergoing widespread renovation and construction.

Transport

LA has few walkable areas and public transport isn't generally efficient, making cars an essential part of daily life. In 2017, there were just under 8 million vehicle registrations in LA county[1]. This car culture is probably why traffic is the second thing people think about when Los Angeles comes to mind - after Hollywood, of course.

Over the last couple of years, the major US tech companies - Facebook, Apple, Amazon, Netflix, and Google - have bought or rented more than 3.35 million square feet in Los Angeles, mostly in Silicon Beach, according to commercial real estate company, Costar. With the rise in tech jobs, more engineering talent is being retained from leading LA universities, such as Caltech, UCLA, and USC, as well as bringing in more external talent.

With the population of LA County increasing from 9.5 million in 2000 to 10.15 million in 2017, and half of that growth coming directly from the City of LA, more people mean more cars, and more cars mean more congestion.

Consumer product delivery is contributing to this increased congestion. With the rise of Amazon and home delivery options in a highly consumer-driven market catering to millions of people, more and more goods are being delivered, which means far more delivery vehicles on the road.

[1] Los Angeles Almanac, Vehicle Registrations Los Angeles County.

In contrast to the traffic problems of the last couple of decades, Los Angeles enjoys a historic position as the original aviation capital of the world: it's also home to the largest ports in the country, and the only airport in the US to rank in the top five for both passenger and cargo traffic.

With these conflicting identities, and more transportation needed for people and goods, it's no wonder that LA has found itself leading the way in innovation when it comes to mobility.

"Like earlier generations of English intellectuals who taught themselves Italian in order to read Dante in the original, I learned to drive in order to read Los Angeles in the original."

Reyner Banham, Architect and Author of Los Angeles: The Architecture of Four Ecologies

City of cars

We all think LA was built for cars but that's not strictly true. Many of the major freeways stem from the city's Spanish roots: El Camino Real down the Californian coast, once marched by Catholic missionaries, is now the Pacific Coast Highway. Many of the wide boulevards were originally fence lines between major ranches. San Vicente, Santa Monica, Rodea - sound familiar? Los Angeles was actually redesigned for cars.

Most Angelenos use cars because they have to. Public transport is available, but, unless you live directly on the routes, travelling by public transport can be slow and laborious. There's also a stigma among the relatively well-off that buses are for people too poor to drive cars. To some degree, that makes sense. If a bus trip takes up to three times longer than another form of transport, the only people who will invest the additional time are those who can't afford an alternative. I've never known any of my friends or colleagues in LA to use the bus system. In fact, only 7 percent of LA County residents account for 80 percent of all bus trips[2].

This car culture is probably why Angelenos spend a whopping 104 hours per week in their cars in peak congestion[3]. This is one set of rankings that LA is not proud to lead, and is a far worse score than that of our northern neighbours in San Francisco, who come in 2nd at 89 hours. The total time spent getting to work isn't that far off the US average, though. In Los Angeles, 13% of people spend more than 60 minutes commuting to work, compared with 9% for the rest of the US. The average commute time is 29 minutes in LA and California, compared with 26 minutes nationally.

[2] LA Metro's Nextgen Bus Study. [3] INRIX Global Congestion Ranking 2016.

A study of mobile phone location data from 5 million people - anonymised, of course, and only accurate within 300m - gave an idea of how they are moving around the city, whatever transport they are using. This data showed that only 16 percent of trips in LA County were longer than 10 miles. Two-thirds of all travel was less than five miles.

So, it seems that the amount of time spent in cars isn't down to the length of the journey: it's the fact that people are sitting in congestion. Perhaps that is why a UCLA survey in 2017 found that dissatisfaction with transportation and traffic ranked as one of the most negative categories.

It makes sense, then, that these vexing problems affecting so many people in the city means that there is significant commitment to finding a solution, turning Los Angeles into an exciting hub for innovation around mobility. Here are some of the key areas of development:

Data, data, data

Seleta Reynolds, General Manager of LADOT, the LA Department of Transport, has been a pioneer in this area, creating a new platform to help manage dockless micro-mobility programmes (see later in the chapter for more on public scooters and electric bikes). This morphed to standardised two-way communication for cities and private companies to share information about their operations. The city can use this data to inform public policy and also for real-time traffic management. It became so popular that the platform was opened up to become the Open Mobility Foundation, which is now used by more than 50 other cities in the US and dozens of others around the world. Imagine if this system could contain all mobility data within a city to give a single holistic view. With that information, a city could start to fully understand what measures need to be taken where, to make transportation easier for all. Best practices could be shared between cities, meaning we can learn from each other and avoid repeating the same mistakes.

Electric is where it's at

California has the highest percentage of electric cars sold in the US in 2018: at 5%, it's almost double the number sold in the next largest state: Washington. Los Angeles has one of the highest shares of electric vehicles in the country. Mayor Garcetti has set a target of 100% electric vehicles by 2050 – a high ambition, but the city is putting its money where its mouth is and aims to convert all city fleet vehicles to zero-emission, where technically feasible, by 2028.

There are two main ways to reach these goals. Firstly, the infrastructure needs to be in place, particularly for charging. The City of LA has committed to installing 400 EV chargers at City buildings, parks, and all libraries, plus 500 additional streetlight EV chargers.

Secondly, there's cost. Consumers may save on fuel by owning an EV, but the upfront cost is high. Since EVs are relatively new, people are buying brand new cars and the second-hand market isn't yet flourishing. Federal rebates exist but depend very much on who is in the White House. California offers a rebate of $2,500-4,500, depending on income.

As part of Mayor Garcetti's own Green New Deal, launched in spring 2019, he has set targets of 100% zero-emission vehicles by 2050 and committed to electrify 100% of Metro and LADOT buses by 2030 to lead by example.

With electric vehicles becoming increasingly popular, the city can also start thinking about introducing zero-emission zones. Los Angeles has committed to having its first one by 2020 as part of the C40 cities around the globe that is committed to taking action on climate change.

Getting public transport right

In 2016, more than 71% of voters approved 'Measure M', with the slogan 'Keep LA moving'. Measure M is a sales tax set to generate $120 billion over 40 years to extend rail and bus services and improve accessibility and infrastructure. The cost is minimal to users - about 2 cents on a $4 coffee.

Most of the money will go on extending the metro lines, though some of the planned expenditure will be used to improve bus and bike lanes, making it easier to use alternative forms of transport and contribute to street improvements (earthquakes and a climate of severe dry/wet extremes do a lot of damage).

Critics suggest that while people support developing the infrastructure, most of them don't actually plan to use it themselves: they want it to take others off the roads to ease congestion. Attitudes will change as public transport becomes more efficient and people's perception of it changes. Watch this space.

Public meets private

The Office of Extraordinary Innovation (OEI) was created in 2015 by LA Metro to 'identify the best ideas in transportation and help to test, refine, and implement them at LA Metro. OEI is focused on finding new ways of thinking and innovative new methods and approaches for bringing convenient, affordable, and effective mobility solutions to Los Angeles.'

Speaking to Dr Joshua Schank, Chief Innovation Officer, one of the things that struck me was his focus on ripping up the rule book of government tenders. After all, the public sector works notoriously slowly by comparison with tech companies. Most government departments operate in a similar way: they identify a problem, write a brief to fix it, send out a Request for Proposal, evaluate the proposals, award the contract to the winning bid, and get to work.

Joshua argues that this process is far too bureaucratic and doesn't always make sense. Firstly, private company executives may have great ideas that are never properly heard because they don't fit into the existing process. He has introduced an 'unsolicited proposal policy' that can jump-start the traditional process or lead to new working models, although the proposals could create an administrative burden. Joshua points out that the policy of open proposals reduces the risks and can decrease overall costs, as well as getting projects to delivery much more quickly.

A theoretical example he gives is enhancing LA County's measure M at city level, encouraging commuters to use public transit by subsidising the cost of shared rides to and from rail stations.

Photo credit: the Boring company

The (anything but) Boring company

We must not forget that the invincible futurist Elon Musk lives in Los Angeles. Although he faces the same traffic congestion as the rest of us, he thinks about things differently. Aside from his space venture, renewable energy work, and Neurolinks, he has also created The Boring Company.

To solve the problem of gridlocked traffic, roads must become 3D – and that means either flying cars or tunnels. Unlike flying cars, tunnels are weatherproof, out of sight, and won't fall on your head. A large network of tunnels, many levels deep, would help alleviate congestion in any city, no matter how large it grew (just keep adding new levels). The key to making this work is increasing tunnelling speed and dropping costs by a factor of 10 or more – which is exactly the goal of The Boring Company.

It has even developed a system that turns the excavated dirt into bricks which can then be sold or used to line the tunnel.

This isn't just theoretical: the first tunnel in LA County, just over a mile long, was completed in December 2018, from SpaceX offices in Hawthorne. There are several other tunnels undergoing permitting and environmental reviews, including one that would take people directly to the Dodgers' Stadium from various LA neighbourhoods.

These tunnels are a precursor to 'Loop' and 'Hyperloop': high-speed underground transportation systems where passengers in pressured pods travel at speeds of 155 and 600+ miles per hour respectively. Of course, we are all waiting with bated breath for these exciting new developments to ease all of our travel woes.

Future Thinking

In Los Angeles, it feels like every other car is a Tesla - another of Elon Musk's inspired innovations which has arguably pushed the car industry straight into the future. One of the features of the car is its self-driving mode. Once this has been refined, proved out, and agreed at regulation level (which may take years, even though Garcetti's Green Deal wants to ensure the city is ready for Autonomous Vehicles (AV) by the 2028 Olympic and Paralympic Games), the impacts on commuting and car ownership are huge.

All cars would be connected to the cloud, feeding routing information for every vehicle. This would enable traffic flows to be automated, making congestion a thing of the past.

If cars can drive themselves, will we still need parking in cities - or will cars simply drive themselves out to larger car parks built on cheaper land? Indeed, is there any point in them idly sitting in car parks when we're not using them? They could be rented out to other passengers, à la Uber. Will we even need to own cars, or could they become yet another on-demand service?

And, if we're not driving ourselves, what will we do with all that extra time? Media companies are already starting to think about how they can dominate the extra time people would have to spare.

In reality, traffic congestion in Los Angeles has to improve. The will is there in every single sector - be it personal, private, or public. The likely scenario is that there won't be a single catalyst for change, but that a combination of the above, potentially with the addition of congestion pricing to deter unnecessary journeys, will slowly improve traffic and get Angelenos out of their gas-guzzling cars.

LA locations: what you need to know

In the same way that the British always talk about the weather, Angelenos talk about traffic and car routes. Here is a handy guide to local geography lingo to ensure you're not lost in that early part of a business meeting when someone is explaining why the traffic made them late:

SoCal
*Southern California
(including Los Angeles and San Diego)*

NoCal
*Northern California
(including San Francisco)*

Silicon Beach
The coastal area between LAX and Santa Monica

Westside
The area west of the 405 Freeway from Brentwood to Malibu down to LAX

LAX
The three-letter code for Los Angeles International Airport

DTLA
Downtown Los Angeles

WeHo
West Hollywood

SaMo
Santa Monica

PCH
Pacific Coast Highway, also known as the 1

The 405
the freeway running north to south, roughly dividing LA into the east side and west side (during busy periods, it's easily mistaken for a giant car park)

The 10
the freeway that crosses the city east to west from Santa Monica through DTLA all the way to Palm Springs and beyond. Do not attempt a trip from Santa Monica eastbound on a Friday afternoon or evening. Ever.

The 110/90/101
If numbers like these are mentioned, especially combined with an eye roll or a look of abject despair, just know that they are freeways and nod your head sympathetically

Geographically desirable
referring to a person or a company that is within a reasonable drive. Someone who is geographically desirable will never live on the opposite side of the 405

Those fantastic/ pesky scooters

One sunny day in Santa Monica in September 2017, electric scooters suddenly appeared on the streets, seemingly from nowhere. There was a simple step-by-step process to ride one for just $1 with a few easy rules - you must have a valid driving licence and wear a helmet, the second rule being largely ignored. The city was captivated by these scooters, with people hopping on them to try one out then using them for short commutes. Anything presented as an alternative to cars – and that traffic! - is generally welcomed in LA, especially as this particular alternative was more environmentally friendly too. I loved them.

Travis VanderZanden, an ex Uber and Lyft executive, launched the scooter company, Bird. With no specific laws in place governing this form of transport, he decided to go down the route of begging for forgiveness after launching, rather than asking the city for permission to launch the scooter programme.

But then complaints started coming in: scooters were littering the pavements, riders were dangerous on the roads, kids were riding tandem. The city of Santa Monica was in a tricky situation because public opinion was so divided on the scooters: people either loved them or hated them.

The local police were directed to ensure that people were following the rules, and to fine those who weren't. One of my friends had a particularly expensive commute to work when she was fined $230 for not wearing a helmet.

Bird's revenue went from $0 to more than $100 million within a year. It became the quickest company to reach a $1 billion valuation, and had doubled that to a $2 billion valuation within a year. Travis' risky plan had paid off.

Another scooter company, Lime, which had launched in another city, also brought their scooters to the streets of Santa Monica.

The city council decided the best way forward was to launch an official trial programme which they put out to tender. This allowed the city to set certain boundaries, including some no-go zones, such as the beach path, and take back some control over how the scooters were distributed. But the bidding process was opaque and the two winning companies were neither of the incumbents. Bird had built a loyal following in Santa Monica, and launched an in-app campaign encouraging its customers to take action. Long story short, Bird, Lime, and several other scooter companies are all operating in Santa Monica - and the city is still divided.

Scooters also play into Mayor Garcettis's Green New Deal for LA City. The deal aims to increase the number of trips made by walking, biking, and micro-mobility (which encompasses scooters, electric bikes, and other forms of shared transit that carry one or two people) by at least 50% by 2035, then to maintain this to 2050.

A scooter trip certainly counts as micro-mobility, but the vehicles do create road traffic. While the scooters themselves are green, the 'Bird Hunters', who have signed up to collect and charge them for a bounty of $5-25, spend their evenings driving around picking up and dropping off scooters at designated places. This contributes to more slow-moving traffic, often cited by critics as an issue.

Bird was behind an emerging global cultural phenomenon. Still based in Santa Monica, the company now operates in dozens of countries around the world and has opened the door to other forms of micro mobility, including Uber's electric 'Jump Bikes'.

The Port of Los Angeles

A whopping 40% of goods consumed in the US have had at least one of their components pass through the Ports of LA or Long Beach at some point during their creation. I learnt this while out on a ship with some of the Port's senior directors, discovering the impact this often underestimated zone has on Los Angeles, California, and the whole of the USA. (Incidentally, it also provided filming locations for A Few Good Men, CSI Miami, and The Wire.)

Photo credit: Port of Los Angeles

The ports of Los Angeles and Long Beach are the largest in the US and two of the biggest in this part of the world. Their size and effect on the economy should not be underestimated. In 2014, a new class of megaship was introduced to Asia-US trade, the increased size of which created more work which unfortunately coincided with a union negotiation that decreased productivity. This created a backlog, leaving ships anchored outside San Pedro Bay. Fixable, yes. But the effect of these delays was so immense that Deutsche Bank's AG Chief, U.S. Economist Joe LaVorgna, predicted it could reduce national GDP by up to 1% in the first quarter of 2015.

Imports into the US are predominantly from Asia. Seasonal goods - including avocados, a Los Angeles staple - arrive from Latin America. Most goods passing through the ports are imports of furniture, auto parts, apparel, footwear, and electronics.

As foreign policy changes, so does the origin of imports. China has historically been a large supplier to the US, but, under President Trump's trade feud, this is changing. Vietnam is suddenly, from nowhere, one of the top three nations from which the US receives imports.

One third of imports are consumed locally and two thirds end up on a train, with much of the freight heading to Memphis, which is close to many car-making companies. Given this mix, it's unsurprising that a new spread of businesses has opened, spanning logistics, trucking, storage fulfilment, and shipping. Companies that have raised capital in the last few years include Next Trucking (a platform connecting shippers with owner/operators and small fleets), Cargomatics (a platform for connecting local shippers and local truckers in real-time), The Dray Alliance (trucking service powered by technology to drive reliability, transparency, and connectivity for containerised freight), and Flowspace (on-demand warehousing for business).

Around the Port of Los Angeles, in the area of San Pedro, is a free-trade zone. This allows components to be assembled before officially arriving in the country, or being transported elsewhere for further assembly. And, while more than half the containers leave the Port of LA empty, the US exports some goods, including paper, animal feed, fabrics and cotton, soybeans, and scrap metal.

The Ports are state assets entrusted to the cities of LA and Long Beach to manage as landlords. Dock space is leased to companies that handle the cargo operations. As a highly unionised industry, operation is not cheap. Several terminals have begun to automate, a costly investment that can deliver extended hours of productivity. The industry is watching to see whether the high initial costs of automation will pay off in savings from long-term efficiency. The Port of Los Angeles has also worked with GE Transportation to develop a cloud-based digital portal that provides real-time cargo data to supply chain stakeholders, so that they can move their goods through the ports in a more predictable and efficient manner.

Another customer of the Port of LA is SpaceX, Elon Musk's space company. One of its unique propositions is that it recovers and reuses rockets wherever possible. The recovery operations of Falcon rockets and Dragon spacecraft are run out of the Port of Los Angeles.

Photo credit: LAX

Los Angeles International Airport (LAX)

If you have ever been through LAX (el-ay-ex), you will have noticed how busy it is. Always. There are more than 700 flights/day at the world's 4th busiest airport. It's also one of the busiest cargo airports in the country.

Built on 35 acres for an original capacity of 35-40 million passengers per year, LAX now serves 89 million. Saying that it's over capacity is an understatement, but with communities and an ocean surrounding the airport, there is no room for expansion.

The owners, Los Angeles World Airports (LAWA), are therefore focusing on improving efficiency to give people a quick, smooth journey. Alongside this, they are re-evaluating the customer experience beyond simply getting people from A to B.

If getting to the airport proves difficult, it can set the mood for an entire trip. This is often a frustration for people taking flights out of LAX. The original design of the horseshoe around the terminal became flawed as traffic increased dramatically. To decentralise this traffic, an automated people carrier (or tram as most of us would know it) is being built. There will be six stops: three in the airport and three outside. One of these stops is likely to be for rideshare, such as Uber and Lyft, which has been the cause of more traffic, yet is now a staple of many people's commute.

At the end of 2017, it was announced that LAX would work with the Transportation Security Administration (TSA) as part of their Innovation Task Force (ITF) to pilot and test airport safety and solutions. The aim? To shorten waiting times and improve guest experience at LAX. Currently, there are two main ways this is being tested:

- By using facial recognition and biometrics to "automate the identification and boarding pass verification process. Travellers who are ticketed on an international flight can opt to use the biometric recognition system to verify their identity."

- Trialling 3D scanning of hand luggage, making it quicker and easier to detect suspicious devices.

In terms of passenger experience, LAX is keeping the airport local, placing LA brands over national retail brands where possible. In the terminals, for instance, you'll find a number of LA specific brands, including Homeboy Cafe, LA Originals, and even a food truck.

For some, LAX is just too much to deal with. So, for celebrities, corporate clients, and anyone else who can afford it, there is a separate terminal which I like to think of as the secret terminal. Instead of sitting in traffic then walking an average of 2,200 steps through the airport's terminals, passengers take just 70 steps, avoiding the crowds and enjoying their own private suite with a food service pantry, a two-person daybed, and a private bathroom. They are then delivered to the gate by private car when it's time to board.

Photo credit: The Private Suite

Photo credit: LAX

LAX's private suites terminal has its own TSA and Border Control for an even smoother transit. Membership and use of the suites on a return international flight would set you back around $10k (including the annual membership). This is not cheap - but not extortionate compared with the cost of a long-haul business or first class flight.

Aerospace: how LA's other bedrock industry came to be

Aerospace is, historically, LA's other major industry, but one that is usually eclipsed by the glitz and glamour of Hollywood. After visiting Google's beautifully remodelled new office, the Spruce Goose, in the heart of Silicon Beach, I was told a fascinating story that explains a lot about the birth of the aerospace industry in Los Angeles, how the city became a major force after WWII, and how that is now central to Google's new Silicon Beach space.

By the time WWII broke out, the aircraft industry already had a foothold in Los Angeles, thanks to a few key people who were active in the early 1900s, including the mechanic brothers the Lougheeds (later changed to Lockheed). They started building a flying boat in their backyard and became leading plane manufacturers during and after the Second World War. One of their first employees, Jack Northrup, a self-taught engineering genius, went on to build one of the most important space companies of today - Northrup Grumman.

LA was a strategic aerospace hub, with oil refineries along the coast from LA to Santa Barbara (one of which was attacked by a Japanese submarine during the war), favourable geographical conditions, cheap land, and access to the large ports of LA and Long Beach.

Amid tensions between the US and Japan, the Pacific became a focal point for the US war effort. With its resources and ideal location – far removed from European targets - Los Angeles became the ideal production hub for military aircraft, war supplies, and ammunition.

Movie mogul and aviation expert Howard Hughes, who was the first person to achieve a round-the-world flight in a Lockheed plane, talked his way into a major government contract to deliver military carrier flying boats as transatlantic transportation during the war. Officially called Hughes H-4 Hercules, but more commonly known as the Spruce Goose, the flying boat cost $23 million (equivalent to more than $250 million today) and was completed after the war, but only managed one very short flight.

The hangar in which it was built is where Google has its incredibly plush offices, complete with a board room mocked up to be identical to the one which existed in Howard Hughes' time.

The media mogul made history and had a huge impact on LA. By the end of the war, the city accounted for 17% of America's total war production. This led to the evolution of a small aircraft industry into a fully-fledged aerospace behemoth. In order to accommodate the physical and economic growth in California for people to live and work, government spending increased from $8 billion a year to $100 billion. LA became the home of Boeing and Northrup Gruman, and is where the Apollo moon module and the space shuttles were built.

Photo credit: JMMJ / Shutterstock.com

Aerospace in the here and now

Until a few years ago, space travel was largely dominated by the US Government, which accounted for approximately 70% of research and development spending in the US until 2013. Since space travel is no longer a national pursuit, it relies on a burgeoning private sector. Startup space companies attracted $2.5 billion in 2017[4]. And, by 2018, government spending accounted for just 40%.

One of the catalysts for private sector space development was the founding of the 'X Prize' in LA. The first of these prizes was funded by Anousheh and Amir Ansari, who offered a prize of $10 million to any non-government agency able to launch a reusable vehicle capable of taking tourists into space. This competition model created an impetus for creative breakthroughs. The prize was won by a company called Tier One in 2004. Since then, more than $140 million has been given in prize money in a number of fields to companies creating industry-changing technologies. When the space sector was government-led, it focused on large-scale and long-duration missions. However, with growing private sector involvement, space has become more service-based. As more companies enter the market, so do shared services, such as manufacturing or launch services. This, in turn, decreases barriers to entry, since startups can pay for just the share they need rather than build out entire facilities.

[4] Space Ventures Coalition 2019

These lower barriers to entry attract more businesses, which fuels a burgeoning startup scene. The effect is so significant that the government has had to align procurement processes to act more like enterprises, so they can more easily buy the new technology and services coming to market.

With the development of these shared new services in recent years, time-to-market has been reduced. It used to take years to get a single satellite from prototype to orbit: now it can be done in a matter of months and for a much lower cost. This is partly due to tech advancements, partly to shared services.

Translating this into numbers, Euroconsult estimates that 7,000 small satellites are due to be launched over the next decade. This compares with just 1,200 over the last decade, 950 of which were in the last five years.

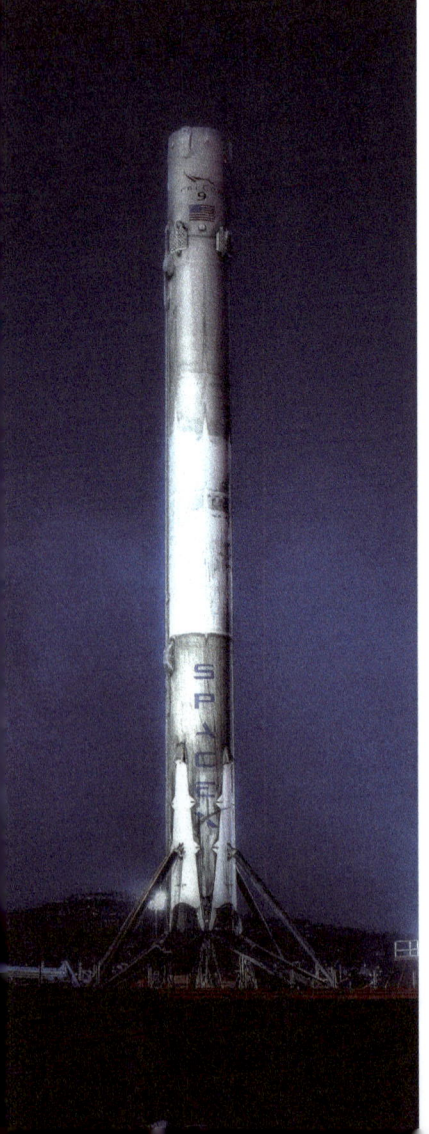

Photo credit: Port of Los Angeles

Los Angeles is not dominated by any one large player, although one of its better-known companies, SpaceX, is also one of the most valuable venture capital-based space startups. Founded in 2002 by Elon Musk, it is part of a public/private partnership with NASA. It was the first commercial company to deliver supplies to the International Space Station, and, in 2017, had no fewer than 18 successful launches. No wonder the company is valued at $25 billion[5].

Space is big business. Elon Musk aside, it has attracted billionaires, including Jeff Bezos and Richard Branson, and the Bank of America Merrill Lynch estimates the business will grow from $339 billion today to $2.7 trillion by 2045. To achieve this valuation, businesses need to work together. To do so, it makes sense for them to be close to each other. So, it's no surprise that they're clustered south of the airport, with a plethora of networking and industry groups.

VCs look out for useful technologies in adjacent industries which might have aerospace applications. For example, some of the technologies being developed in and around Los Angeles include health, where instruments collect data to help humans make the best decisions; transport, where automation and AI are at the heart of developments in self-driving cars; and Hollywood, where visual effects are used to model real-life scenarios. Again, having multiple industries in close proximity is beneficial to the overall ecosystem: technologies are no longer siloed by industry.

[5] Data from Space Ventures Coalition 2019

TL;DR

- Los Angeles is leading the way with its Open Mobility Data Foundation. Other cities are following in its footsteps, using the framework set by LA to understand mobility across a range of transport.

- There is an urgent need to innovate given LA's notorious traffic jams, and a number of startups are basing themselves in Los Angeles to meet this demand. They include novel innovators, such as Elon Musk's The Boring Company, which is tunnelling underground in search of radical new solutions.

- Electric scooters have been a huge hit in LA, with Bird being the fastest company ever to reach a $1 billion valuation. However, regulations need to catch up to create a structure for use that can be agreed within communities.

- No single solution will solve the traffic problem, but a combined approach offering different solutions as a carrot, and possible congestion charges as a stick, is likely to ease traffic in the near future.

- Little known by many in the city, the Ports of LA and Long Beach are a vital part of the US economy. As the largest container ports in the US, 40% of consumer goods have at least one component come through one of the ports during their creation.

- Natural resources, combined with talent in design and technology, have made LA a leader in the aerospace industry, where it continues to innovate.

- The aerospace industry is no longer government-led: it's become a private initiative, with funding provided by well-known billionaires and venture capitalists.

Conclusion

So where next?

Los Angeles is going from strength to strength. Is it the new Silicon Valley? No, nor should it try to be. Instead, LA has its own set of outstanding credentials.

Entertainment and aerospace have been LA's bedrock industries for more than a century. Now the city is blazing a trail in exciting contemporary industries, such as gaming, cannabis transportation, biotech, and wellness. Los Angeles excels at the intersection of new and existing industries, all of them feeding and fuelling each other.

The city attracts smart, creative people who tend to try new ways to do things rather than rely on tried-and-tested models: it's a diverse place that thrives on reinventing itself for the better. Yet, for its size, the startup and innovation community is still small and intimate enough to create genuine collaboration and build a strong sense of a shared destiny.

The cost of living in Los Angeles is still significantly cheaper than Silicon Valley and New York, and is not subject to the same geographical constraints, making property prices more reasonable and therefore an attractive long-term prospect for individuals and businesses alike. Glorious sunshine, miles of white sandy beaches, and a thriving food and drinks scene make the LA lifestyle hard to beat.

Conclusion

Over the last decade, the startup ecosystem has been growing and now provides all the funding, talent, and resources the city needs to be independent. But, as independent as it is, there is a natural, symbiotic relationship between Los Angeles and Silicon Valley that I believe will continue to develop, with each place carving out its own future.

Los Angeles wants to be a city of the future and is doing everything it can to get there. Securing major national and international events - the Superbowl in 2020, the 2023 US Open, the FIFA World Cup in 2026, and the 2028 Olympics - will help secure its place on the world stage.

With money flowing into the city, we'll see how LA both welcomes and protects itself against the gentrification that this rapid change can bring. And all eyes will be on whether Mayor Garcetti can continue his push for public-private partnerships to drive the city forward and achieve his green ambitions for LA.

Anyone who is culturally curious and interested in business innovation would be foolish to ignore Los Angeles.

I, for one, can't wait to see how the city develops, and feel even more optimistic about the future of Los Angeles than I did when I started this book. There is an infectious enthusiasm among those like me who have made LA their home, and all of us are passionate about playing our part in making it bigger, brighter, and more fabulous than it already is. But, don't take my word for it: come and see for yourself...

About the author

Jodie Hopperton is a British media executive based in Los Angeles.

In a career spanning more than 15 years, she has worked with technology startups in addition to corporate roles with Trinity Mirror and the New York Times. She has also worked with nonprofits such as the World Association of Newspapers and the Global Editors Network.

She lived in Paris, Madrid, and London before moving to Los Angeles in 2015, where she founded FORE:media in the belief that Los Angeles has become every bit as inspiring as Silicon Valley – probably more so.

FORE:media helps executives in Los Angeles and other US cities place themselves at the heart of the ever-shifting business environment and at the vanguard of innovation. The company helps these executives acquire the knowledge and tools needed to build and adapt strategies by meeting the change-makers in person, connecting, and collaborating with technology and innovation leaders. FORE:media has arranged executive level tours in Los Angeles for clients ranging from Boston Consulting Group to the Global Editors Network.

Realising that Los Angeles isn't an easy city to understand, Jodie wrote this book to demystify it and convey to the wider world the scale and depth of the innovation taking place there.

Acknowledgements

This book would not have been possible without the more than 100 executives who took time to share with me their personal journeys as well as their expert views on business, industry and how Los Angeles is changing.

I owe huge thanks to the people who either validated or argued with my views and assumptions, enabling me to get under the skin of LA to find out what makes this unusual city tick.

To enable a deep dive into a subject and stimulate layered and complex discussion, several companies were generous in co-hosting roundtables: most notably Sally Drexler from Odgers Berndtson, Julie Chappell and James Cummings at London & Partners, Klay Nichol, Gloria Chang Yip, Bob Graziano at JP Morgan Private Bank.

Several of Los Angeles' skilled connectors opened up their networks for me. In particular, I'd like to thank Holly Gottlieb, Brian Schwartz, Beatriz Acevedo, Mitch Berman and Stephen Cheung.

Agency TK, in particular Nicole Levings and Olivia Nicholson, went to great lengths to create a design which reflects the nuances of the city.

Lastly, but importantly, I sometimes thought I may have bitten off more than I could chew while working on this book. I was lucky to have endless sources of encouragement, not least from my fantastic husband Lippe Oosterhof, who continued to reinforce that this was a story which needs to be told.

LA
RE:

www.ingramcontent.com/pod-product-compliance
Lightning Source LLC
Chambersburg PA
CBHW062026290426
44108CB00025B/2791